Praise for

"I've read hundreds of self-[help books?] only a handful are incisive, beautifully written, and genuinely comforting. *Learning to Trust Yourself* is one of these rare treasures. Tama Kieves combines a gentle heart with a keen intellect and visionary worldview. She brings all three to each page, offering the guidance and support we all need in these turbulent times."
—Martha Beck, *New York Times* bestselling author of *Finding Your Own North Star* and *Steering by Starlight*

"In a world where external validation often drowns out our inner voice, *Learning to Trust Yourself* emerges as a beacon of clarity. This book is a spiritual roadmap for those seeking to unlock their highest potential by cultivating unwavering trust in the wisdom within. Transcend the noise of doubt and embrace the deep, intuitive knowing that is your birthright. A transformative read for anyone ready to step boldly into their purpose."
—Michael B. Beckwith, founder and CEO of Agape International Spiritual Center, author of *Life Visioning* and *Spiritual Liberation*

"*Learning to Trust Yourself* is a brilliant guide to honoring yourself and uncovering your inner strength to create your dreams. With humor, honesty, and practical exercises, Tama Kieves gives you a roadmap to authentic confidence and your ultimate potential. I recommend you read this book right now! —Marci Shimoff, *New York Times* bestselling author of *Happy for No Reason*

"The power-packed pages in *Learning to Trust Yourself* will result in your being able to actually live in the ways you've dreamed of. This book is an indispensable guide." —SARK, artist and bestselling author of *Succulent Wild Woman* and *Make Your Creative Dreams Real*

ALSO BY TAMA KIEVES

Learning to
Trust
Yourself

❖❖❖❖❖❖❖❖❖❖❖❖❖❖❖❖❖❖❖❖❖❖❖❖❖❖❖❖

Breaking Through the Blocks
That Hold You Back

❖❖❖❖❖❖❖❖❖❖❖❖❖❖❖❖❖❖❖❖❖❖❖❖❖❖❖❖

TAMA KIEVES

ST. MARTIN'S
ESSENTIALS
NEW YORK

The information in this book is not intended to replace the advice of the reader's own physician or other medical professional. You should consult a medical professional in matters relating to health, especially if you have existing medical conditions, and before starting, stopping, or changing the dose of any medication you are taking. Individual readers are solely responsible for their own health-care decisions. The author and the publisher do not accept responsibility for any adverse effects individuals may claim to experience, whether directly or indirectly, from the information contained in this book.

First published in the United States by St. Martin's Essentials, an imprint of St. Martin's Publishing Group

LEARNING TO TRUST YOURSELF. Copyright © 2025 by Tama Kieves. All rights reserved. Printed in the United States of America. For information, address St. Martin's Publishing Group, 120 Broadway, New York, NY 10271.

www.stmartins.com

Designed by Steven Seighman

Library of Congress Cataloging-in-Publication Data

Names: Kieves, Tama J., author.
Title: Learning to trust yourself : breaking through the blocks that hold you back / Tama Kieves.
Description: First edition. | New York : St. Martin's Essentials, 2025.
Identifiers: LCCN 2024041775 | ISBN 9781250355515 (trade paperback) | ISBN 9781250355522 (ebook)
Subjects: LCSH: Self-actualization (Psychology) | Self-reliance.
Classification: LCC BF637.S4 K498 2025 | DDC 158.1—dc23/eng/20241023
LC record available at https://lccn.loc.gov/2024041775

Our books may be purchased in bulk for promotional, educational, or business use. Please contact your local bookseller or the Macmillan Corporate and Premium Sales Department at 1-800-221-7945, extension 5442, or by email at MacmillanSpecialMarkets@macmillan.com.

First Edition: 2025

10 9 8 7 6 5 4 3 2 1

I dedicate this book to all the salmon, those of us who are compelled to listen to an inner direction even when we doubt ourselves. To the trust warriors—those who love and respect themselves enough to honor their indispensable light.

To all creatives, scientific explorers, conscious industry leaders, trailblazers, lovers of humanity, and messengers, those who walk into the unknown wilderness and recover the holy grail. And to the young woman in me who journaled to her inner teacher and followed her instincts.

May every soul salmon find their way home.

Homecoming is reclaiming who you really are—you are one for whom nothing is impossible when you listen to your truth, and you trust yourself.

Contents

Everything is different when I'm different.

My challenges do not disappear. But now they are not wrecking balls or deal-breakers. They show up as *reminders to go deeper into trusting myself,* trusting my connection to a mysterious good—and to open yet again into the complex wonder of my life.

There are two ways to live. One is to think about everything that could go wrong or is going wrong. The other is to practice listening to a reassuring intelligence within me, a life-giving wisdom that is precise and immediate. I want to live my life from this identity—*the one that is whole and guided.* I don't think I am really living life when I am not living from this identity. I don't think any of us are.

—*Tama Kieves*

Learning to
Trust
Yourself

An Introduction and *Initiation*

WHY TRUSTING YOURSELF IS
THE MEANING OF YOUR LIFE

I am going to tell you all about the messy, outrageous path of listening to myself in this lifetime. I will teach you everything I know. But first I want to just maybe throw this glass of water in your face. With absolute love, of course . . .

I want to startle you out of the same old, same old.

Right now, someone is robbing you—stealing days from your life. Can you imagine? Like an undiagnosed disease this person is eating away months you might have had, maybe years. This isn't an over-dramatization. It's a wake-up call . . . to step into living your life on fire, with gobs of appreciation, meaning, passion, and guaranteed inner peace. Because when you're not trusting yourself, the wacko-crazy person who is stealing the days from your life—is you.

I know what it's like to not trust yourself. Oh my God, I have second-guessed myself, doubts badgering me like nervous kids, hand-wringing grandmothers, and blowhards in the back row. Then I started learning how to listen to myself and to the truth of what I know. That's a brand-new day. I want that day for you, and weeks and months and years. Soar instead of hesitate. Love your life now instead of waiting for some other time.

When you don't trust yourself, you are not using your higher resources—not in the way you can. It's as though there's a kink in your garden hose, and the water can't gush all the way through. No one can live an exceptional life on a squirt or a trickle, though some of us actually think that holding ourselves back is a winning move.

You may doubt the genius and instruction of your own life-force. But I don't. I've seen what happens when we trust our power. You have no idea what you can accomplish when you are in your zone and undiluted.

Life doesn't just have to happen however it happens. You are a conscious being—and there's a reason for that. You have a wild light inside you that can alter any circumstance. Wouldn't it be amazing to learn how?

Sure, you think you have to be "realistic." Not go all gung ho positive mindset or "spiritual" in our metric-centered, material, madhouse world. I get it. I went to Harvard Law School. Enough said. Who wants to be bizarre or a Pollyanna? You don't want to be wrong. And you definitely don't want to be the one caught with your rainbow pants down, clutching your crystals and instant manifestation kit.

But you are putting a kink in your garden hose. You are telling yourself it's safer to listen to others than it is to listen to yourself. You are voting to trust the masses instead of your instincts, your knowing heart, your Yabba-Dabba-Do-Divine Intelligence, or whatever you call a revelation of bulletproof information.

Maybe you waver, trust your connection to brave intuitive forces only some of the time. You tell yourself you are being "responsible." Preventing disappointments.

Yet in the name of intelligence, you are blunting your *highest intelligence*. Because a part of you senses there is another way. *There is your path.* There is the way this life is meant to work for you.

Here's what not trusting yourself and telling yourself to be "realistic" can mean:

You are unconsciously training your eyes and ears to look for a more limited identity than the infinite energy within you. You are acclimating to an image of yourself as helpless or held back by "how things work." You are feeding this image. You are creating that world. Over and over.

Still, it doesn't feel right. A diluted life is not a life you love.

Things may feel familiar—but they don't feel *right*.

There is a hunger to be whole, to not deny your instincts, but to become the person you dream of being. You know there is more to you and more for you. You *know* it.

Even when you try to ignore it, the tug of yearning will not go away. It's always there. This isn't a delusion or some fairy tale. It's a *knowing*. This is the voice of inner guidance. You crave the feeling of being *the real you*. It's your birthright. Your blueprint. Your inner salsa. Your code.

Your life purpose is to listen to your inner voice—but to listen to the voice of love inside yourself instead of the voice of fear. The voice of strength instead of the voice of weakness. This is the paradigm shift. This is how you step into a new identity—and *a true relationship with yourself* and a responsively alive Universe.

Why not commit to living your exceptional life? I invite you to stop following mediocre thinking—and to trust the integrity of your love and knowing instead. Explore your power at a different level. Say yes to your own originality, intelligence, and connection. Dare to have the adventure of your lifetime.

You will do this by learning to trust yourself. I will tell you that there is already a path within you. I will remind you that you have *guidance*. I will remind you that *there is always something working*.

Yet you will need to trust yourself and your exceptional way— all the way.

Here's what that might look like: You will move in the direction of phenomenal instinct. You will not swallow your impulses or truth. You will not collect evidence of lack but evidence of quantum leaps, love, and support. You will *finally be on your own side,* the conductor, choreographer, and press agent of your own possibilities tour. This is how you eat awe for breakfast and ride momentum that arises of itself. Can you imagine that? I can.

Exceptional Focus Creates Exceptional Results

The right focus lights up circuits in your brain and energy you didn't know you had. Perspective changes your world. Trusting yourself is a focus like none other: **You learn to stop diminishing yourself. You unlearn every assumption that weakens or dilutes your genius and vitality.**

And, maybe, just maybe, you love your own being in a way that empowers you to accomplish damn near anything you desire.

I would love you to leave this planet with no regrets. Freedom in your veins. Seashells in your pocket. Humming or wailing out the note of your lifetime, a stream of contribution in your wake. We can create with sacred powers or something like it while in real time. We can experience *real time,* magic, optimization, and homecoming—and the time of our lives.

This is what it means to trust yourself deeply. This can be learned. This can be practiced. And that is what I offer you in this book.

BECOMING YOUR OWN SACRED ALLY

One thing I've learned: **Life reflects back to us the conversation we have within ourselves.** We enter a different room, a new quantum field, a brand-new world . . . when we make different decisions about who we are.

Your life wobbles—because you wobble.

All my life I thought that if just set up the outside of my life to look a certain way, then I could bask in a sense of success, happiness, or being special. But I had the equation wrong.

I fell for the backward twisted promise we've all been sold: the right life will give you the right feeling. I am seeing now that *the right feeling about myself* awakens the right life. No matter what.

I have gotten this far in life even through self-doubt. Self-diminishment. Self-comparison.

But what if I banked on my own design—without hesitation or perpetual evaluation?

What if I *celebrated* my instincts—instead of muffling them?

What if I trusted just one voice within?

What if it was the voice of my Inspired Self . . . an unwavering vote of strength and love?

How would it be to live with a walloping *yes* resounding through the hallways of my being?

This much I know: I am the only person I will spend my entire lifetime with, every single breath, maybe even for eternity.

It's time to stop fighting with myself and weakening my enthusiasm. It's time to start fighting *for* myself and the truth I know. It's my time to bow down to my inner guardian and rise up, with all that I am—singing a hymn of wholeness.

I will become my own sacred ally, my own brilliant guru—the champion of my lifetime, a rainmaker. I wish this for you too.

Because, really, being exceptional is just being unwilling to hobble your own life.

WELCOME TO YOUR EXCEPTIONAL LIFE

I am so grateful you are here. I'm holding the vision of you in your
ideal life—as I sip orange ginger mint tea and write these words.
I have a sense that you and I have met at just the right time. This
book is a coaching session, a training ground, or a flight lesson if
you like. You have extraordinary powers. You know that. I know
that. This work can help you unlock them.

**The Choice: You can get in your own way—*or discover your
own way.***

I had to write this book. In New York City subway stations, you
might see signs that say, "If you see something, say something."
Well, I've seen something, and I keep seeing it.

It started with my own reality-altering career and life transformation (more on that later). I have observed a critical dynamic
through decades of leading others to tap into their astonishing inner powers and create the life and work they love. Through my
books, retreats, online programs, and coaching practice, I've taught
and coached thousands worldwide. Here's what I continue to see.

People who don't succeed *get in their own way.*
People who do succeed *discover their own way.*

There is one crucial factor that moves the dial. Every time. It's
self-trust.

The people who *discovered their own way* didn't waste time
doubting themselves, making themselves wrong, or thinking everyone else had better answers or better lives. These mavericks learned
how to listen to themselves, coax themselves into greatness, find
stamina, self-forgiveness, and take inspired actions. They became

their own allies and partnered with an inner power that altered everything. They touched magic. They trusted—*in their own brand of magic.* Huzzah!

SELF-TRUST IS A PATH

This book will help you walk this path so that you can move past the most common blocks—or ways you get in your own way. With each self-trusting instruction, you will open to a more intentional way to live. Get ready to feel more instinctively alive . . . and more on track in your life.

YOUR BLOCK IS YOUR PORTAL

Why look at the blocks instead of the steps to trusting yourself? Here's why. I bet you know that if you want to lose weight you should eat more kale than lasagna. So how come millions of motivated individuals don't do it? Because real change doesn't happen when we are told what to do.

Real change happens when our blocks are removed.

When we change our beliefs about ourselves and our lives, we can do anything.

That's why I started looking at what blocked people from creating the lives they desired. Most of my clients and students thought their block was an external circumstance like health, money, time, or bad habits. But it was never about that. It was always about what they believed, what they told themselves about themselves, that made all the difference.

Yes. The right relationship to yourself changes everything.

That's why we're going to look at the most common and unconscious ways you stop yourself from trusting your inner genius and spirit. We're going to undo those limits. Remember, wherever you're getting in your own way, there's secret energy. Your "block" is your portal.

YES, EVEN YOUR LIFE IS FLAWLESS

Your life might not look like anything you think you desire. That doesn't mean for a minute that higher genius isn't streaming through your every circumstance. You may get stuck on "the picture" of your life, but your soul is on a bigger adventure.

You can use any circumstance to open to your one wild, true path.

Because here's the thing. You can't know the way to an *inspired* life, or to an exceptional outcome. You can, however, know a relationship with your own spectacular internal guidance. This is the only step you really need.

A BIT ABOUT ME, IN CASE YOU'RE WONDERING . . .

I started writing books, coaching, and leading retreats because I wanted to help others discover and live the life that was calling them. My personal metamorphosis began in the realm of finding my life's work.

Years ago, I changed my career. Really, I shapeshifted. I walked out of one world, *one way of being in the world,* and into another stratosphere.

Let me back up. When I was young, I wanted to be a writer. But everyone "knows" that creative people don't make money. My New York City orthodox Jewish family, school guidance counselors, and maybe the whole freaking East Coast pressed me to be practical. I got "real" and went to law school. Harvard Law School, as "real" as it gets. I graduated with honors and a muted heart.

I landed on the partnership track of a chic law firm, and things appeared peachy. Too bad that inside me, vultures were circling and pecking at me day and night—because they know a dead thing when they see it—even if the dead thing is wearing very nice earrings and lipstick.

I was living a life that wasn't my life—and that isn't living. Truth will always call us to alignment. **Sometimes the call makes itself known through pain.**

In wild pain, I did the unthinkable. I walked out of everything I knew. Without a plan. With not much money, but with a small festive hope in my heart. It was the most important thing I have ever done in my life.

I've written a good deal about my career transition in my other books and about the miraculous journey of trusting myself and getting my first book, *This Time I Dance! Creating the Work You Love,* published. There are some career-transition stories in this book too—because what I learned from changing my career and my identity is universal, and let's just say, phenomenal. These mind-bending principles apply to *any kind of change.*

And in this book, I laser-focus on creating the kind of relationship with yourself that frees you to shift anything—and everything.

In the middle of my transformation, I had to find my own direction and answers. I was living with assumptions about what I could have. Or who I was and what was possible. I began to realize that maybe there's *a different reality* I could know by listening to *a different self,* my Inspired Self.

I'm still on this journey of self-discovery and creating the ever-expanding life of my dreams. I will be learning how to trust myself and the limitlessness within for the rest of my life. I invite you to join me. I look forward to sharing this territory of absolute wonder with you.

A TOUR OF THIS BOOK AND YOUR
SELF-GUIDED JOURNEY

Trust yourself when you read this book. Some of you are grasshoppers. You might prefer to hop around. You can dive into the chapter that grabs your attention right now. Go for it, rebel wonder!

Each chapter might be like taking a one-on-one workshop with me. Take the workshop you need, even if it's "not in order." Your instincts are the real order. You can even read each chapter or teaching piece as a daily meditation. I've intentionally written each piece to stand alone (though they all amplify one another).

Now, there's another way to experience this book. You can follow the self-guided journey that lies within these pages, engaging in the practices, inquiries, and exercises. This book will take you where you want to go—though it may do that in ways you might not expect.

When I teach, I share the deeper nuances of application, or what I call facets of the diamond. So, think of this book as a prism because truth is never a flat or one-size-fits-all concept. You'll find seven sections, each focusing on a dominant block to trusting yourself. Each section has four or five bite-sized chapters that explore different angles of the block and how to experience a specific break-through.

Here's a map of the journey:

1. **THE BLOCK AND THE BREAKTHROUGH:** Before each section, this is your overview of how the chapters that follow will help you trust yourself.
2. **THE PRACTICE:** The heart of the teaching—hold it in your awareness as you read and then see how this practice shows up in your life.
3. **THE TEACHING:** My words and your inner knowing will have a conversation. Absorb the message in the story. You will hear what you need to hear.
4. **SELF-TRUST INQUIRY:** At the end of the piece, a guided reflection helps you apply the realizations you've just experienced.
5. **SELF-TRUST-ISMS:** Pivotal points from the chapter. Self-Trust-isms make great art or journal prompts, and cues for discussion and meditation.
6. **KICKSTARTS AND PRACTICES:** These exercises help you uncover deeper direction and breakthroughs.
7. **ADDITIONAL RESOURCES:** You'll find the **Self-Trust Codes—The Power 15** at the end of this introduction. These are principles you can revisit whenever you need some guidance. At the end of the book, you'll find ways to connect with me via social media for daily tips and inspiration. Finally, I have put together a special collection of videos, meditations, and other material as a gift to enhance this book and your life. I encourage you to experience the **Trust Yourself Mega Pack**, as it's filled with invaluable tools to help you increase self-trust and

live your exceptional life. **Download it for free on page 312.** Or download it now to amplify your experience of reading this book.

About the Stories in This Book

I write from personal experience. I share pretty damn intimately. Maybe you will wonder, *Why is she telling me so much about her ex-boyfriend or hiring an assistant?* It's the way I teach. I've seen that in workshops, participants experience more "ahas" (and laughter) when I share stories combined with teaching points. We are social and nosy animals. We retain stories and examples far more than facts or instructions. Stories *help you feel* or experience a paradigm shift—moving information into transformation.

Plus, you may relate to me. You may even find it "inspiring" that it has taken me so many of these stories to learn what I'm sharing with you. Clearly, there is hope for everyone.

You may notice I repeat certain themes. Even certain aspects of stories. It's not because I've forgotten what I've already written. No, I'm not that bad yet. Rather, I bang the same drum more than once because we learn through repetition.

Also, since readers might jump around in the book and read things out of order, each piece is designed to stand on its own. To do that, I sometimes put in information that was in another chapter because I don't want to assume you've already read it.

All my stories are true. But particularly when I talk about my clients, I have changed names and identifying details to protect their privacy. I also do this with some of my former romances or even minor aspects of my own experience. The essential truth remains the same.

The Teachings of *A Course in Miracles* in This Book

A Course in Miracles is a spiritual mindset–training program. It's a book that has been loved by millions worldwide. It's main teaching is living in love instead of fear. In this book, I use a number of concepts from *A Course in Miracles*. I am sharing the concepts liberally because I've studied and taught this earth-shattering intelligence for decades and it's what I know. I'm not proselytizing. There will be no goat killing or joining of cults.

I found *A Course in Miracles*, or it found me, just when I was desperately looking to feel more secure in life. A boyfriend at the time had told me it would help me succeed in my writing, business, and life. He was right. But then this path to my deeper self became my life. I am still in awe. It's like a supernatural vine in a fairy tale that took over my garden—and my heart.

Honestly, I still think it's crazy that *this* is the spiritual path that grabbed me. I'm Jewish by birth and image-conscious by training, so I would have preferred the kind of mindset training *The New York Times* would highlight. Or something hip like a trip to Nepal and a bald guru with a complicated name and a mantra. Even after all these years of studying *A Course in Miracles*, I am still not at home with the masculine or religious-sounding language. But the essence of the work continues to rock my world. That's why I've felt called to take the genius of it and make it more accessible to others.

Just for clarification's sake, *A Course in Miracles* is not a religion. Also, this spiritual mindset training does not exclude any other path to healing. *A Course in Miracles* says in its preface: "Its only purpose is to provide a way in which some people will be able to find their own Internal Teacher." There you have it.

BEGIN YOUR QUEST: STOP THINKING, START TRUSTING

What would you do *if you knew* you could trust yourself and a Source of loving intelligence in your life? **How about this: For one month, live as though you *do* trust yourself in every situation.**

Take the concepts of this book and test them out—by using them, not by analyzing them.

Only listen to an inner voice that speaks to you with kindness and authority.

Live as though you're always making the right decisions.

Your experience will teach you more than your questions.

This is the quest.

Activation Is More Powerful than Consideration

I spent most of my life in my head, considering ideas, rather than opening wide to experience. As a former attorney, I am *trained* to look for liabilities. My mind is a black-ops beast that can anticipate calamity when everyone else is basking in sunshine, stargazing, and picking blueberries. Shockingly, these skills are not at all compatible with trusting yourself to live an inspired life.

The inspired life is *experiential*. It is not something we can figure out or nail down.

An inspired life works when we move forward, not when we think about moving forward. We will never answer our questions *before* stepping into the adventure. It's the adventure that answers our questions. That's why I had to learn how to go from being a questioner to a quester—someone who engages in the quest for her own answers.

Maybe you'll relate to this. I was afraid to trust myself because I was terrified of being disappointed. I was afraid to believe in a "positive energy" or "Universe" or any idea that made me feel warm inside. I didn't want to break my own heart. I could point to times in my life where I believed something would work and it didn't. I didn't want to open myself up to ever being disappointed again.

Here's what I know now . . . a truth that feels like a meteor shower or like a key to a door that had always been locked:

It wasn't disappointment that caused me to stop believing.

It's when I stopped believing that I felt disappointed.

Yes, things happened that didn't go the way I expected or desired. Then I chose to stop trusting. I closed my heart. Gave up on everything. This self-abandonment sabotaged my frame of mind, my enthusiasm, and my actions. I became unavailable to anything progressing and maturing into better outcomes. *This* was the problem, the cause of my black hole.

Because here's the real truth: Every time I have stayed open and moved forward . . . *continuing to believe in my path* . . . I have discovered something that made me believe in my path.

Begin Your Quest

So, let's begin. This is your mystical petri dish, your personal adventure. You don't need to do this perfectly. Just start. Starting now is how you ignite your exceptional life.

THE SELF-TRUST CODES

The Self-Trust Codes are the principles for living your exceptional life. They are the distilled essence of this book. You can always return to these codes to find the code that you need in your life in any and every given moment.

Note: If you would like a free, beautifully designed download-able copy of these Self-Trust Codes, get them by signing up for your free **Trust Yourself Mega Pack** at the end of the book.

THE SELF-TRUST CODES—THE POWER 15

1. The right relationship to myself changes everything.
2. I hear the voice of self-genius when I stop listening to the voice of self-negation.
3. I see more of what I look for. I focus on the evidence of abundance in my life.
4. When I love what is in front of me, everything comes to me.
5. I give up the thoughts of where I think I should be. I am on a journey that's never been lived before.
6. I craft my perspective because my perspective becomes my world.
7. There is no static reality. Everything shifts when I do.
8. My desires are holy. I have them for a reason. I follow my breadcrumbs.
9. I give myself permission to be in process. Clarity comes from process.
10. I am in the right life. I am guided. I am making the absolute best choices I can make at this time.
11. If there wasn't something here for me, I wouldn't be here. *Magic is here.*
12. I have a trajectory, and something always works. *Something always works.*

13. I go beyond casual belief. I end the weakness of waffling. I leap.

14. I show up with patience. I stop *resisting* difficulty. I move beyond my history.

15. I side with my light. I side with who I know I can be. I dismiss other possibilities.

And for extra credit: I choose to be a presence of love. I bring the frequency of goodwill into the room.

PART I

From Self-Criticism to Self-Love

ACTIVATING YOUR GENIUS

THE BLOCK: Self-Criticism

THE BREAKTHROUGH: *The Voice of Self-Love*

YOU GET IN YOUR OWN WAY
when you listen to the inner voice of self-criticism.

YOU DISCOVER YOUR OWN WAY
when you listen to the inner voice of self-love.

You may not trust yourself because you're listening to a voice of self-criticism that derails you. Of course, it croaks it's just "bettering" you. *You're really a loser,* it reminds you. Best not to invest in happy thoughts. Stay sharp and do *not* love yourself—if you hope to get ahead. But this archaic methodology creates a lesser life.

When you negate yourself, you sabotage your ability to hear the genius within you.

Trusting yourself is about championing your own life. I invite you to experience a brand-new relationship with yourself. Because what if self-love isn't just buying expensive soaps?

Get ready to open the floodgates of creativity, happiness, equilibrium, and even a relationship with the power of the Universe. The voice of self-love within offers advanced technology.

If you aim to create an exceptional life you love, then choose the best inner guide in town. Because the quality of the voice you listen to inside yourself decides the quality of your life.

In this section, we jump into how to champion your own life.

Becoming a Champion
of Your Own Life

THE PRACTICE: The voice you listen to inside yourself determines your entire life. You may have a harsh inner voice. You may think this voice is practical or realistic and will help you get ahead. Yet it's holding you back. Because when you trust the voice of love within you, you awaken a new world. **Your practice is to try on the idea that self-love will not make you weak.** Open to this new form of strength.

True freedom is a conscious, everyday spiritual adventure. It's a reinvention. It's a wholly new relationship with yourself.
—TAMA KIEVES, from *A Year Without Fear*

You're always with yourself,
so you might as well enjoy the company.
—DIANE VON FURSTENBERG

One of the first self-help-type workshops I ever went to was called Self-Love. I had no idea what that meant. I had a hidden fantasy that maybe the teacher would encourage me to eat more Chinese food. "Order lo mein," she'd whisper with guttural authority.

Maybe she would help me see an inner aurora borealis or forgive myself for not marrying a rich cardiologist and making my parents beam. Or maybe I'd finally stop feeling crazy restless or stuck inside myself. But no, the workshop leader droned on about counting your breaths or cleansing your chakras. I lost interest. Maybe I went out and got egg rolls.

I look back now and realize that even way back then, I knew on some level that I needed to give myself permission to make radically new choices. To wake up and be truly free. I needed to bust out of the small life that self-judgment was creating for me. I needed relief from the rabid taskmaster in my head dominating my attention: *You're not doing enough. You should be further ahead. What's wrong with you? Everyone else knows what to do. You're a loser.*

At the time I thought that if I trusted myself to do what I really wanted in any given moment, I'd ruin my life. It never dawned on me that denying my intuition and closing my heart to myself *was* ruining my life.

I had no idea that I was holding myself back from my own birthright. I didn't know that if I could let go of my inner criticism, I'd liberate my fire and wild well-being. I had no clue that self-judgment was blocking the floodgates of creativity, wealth, equilibrium, and even a relationship with the juju power of the Universe. Besides, I had no idea *how* to let go of this controlling inner voice.

I didn't yet know that no amount of driven achievement would make me happy. I hadn't yet discovered that I would always hunger to feel connected to myself, and to a sense of *something more*, a Presence, a crazy love energy, and the feeling that all was right in the marrow of my bones.

Self-love? I thought it was an ad campaign for artisan candles made of beeswax. I imagined hedonists or wan, droopy people reassuring one another, "You deserve love," and the others saying, "No, no, you do." Really, I was clueless. I had no idea what loving yourself meant.

Many years ago, I dated a thin, long-haired, tarot-card-reader boyfriend—not exactly a corporate lawyer, Lexus-driving achievement freak. We strolled along at an outdoor art and food festival in Denver's Civic Center Park. He bought me a calligraphy print that read, "Be Gentle with Yourself." I was a young, Harvard Law School–trained litigator in a top law firm at the time. I was hot shit. Only I felt like crap. Lost. Like I was in someone else's life. Drowning. I was not "in alignment" with my desires, values, or my chakras.

A wildly loving inner voice gives rise to a life you wildly love.

I came from an alpha-centric world. So I held up the "Be Gentle with Yourself" print as though it might be coated with anthrax, or worse than that, *baby powder.* It just sounded hokey. Like, eat lollipops. Pretend you're happy. Don't forget to sing in the rain.

"Really?" I said to him and smirked. "Yeah, really," he said. And he said it with authority, like a kick to the solar plexus, like some inner kung fu master stunning me with heat. That was the first time I considered that love might be a form of strength. That it might even be a portal to another life. I felt unsteady. I also felt intrigued.

However, I was afraid of my desire to feel good. I was afraid to believe in a Universe that loved me—or that good things could really happen *for me.* I was afraid that these kinds of beliefs would trick me or slow my progress. Would I just live in a fantasy and forget to take action? I already felt so behind. I was always trying to catch up to an image of myself that seemed so much better than I was.

Enter the paradigm shift. Because it is love that revolutionized the playing field.

I had no idea that I was screaming for my own support. A shred of self-allegiance or of rooting for myself. A thimble of self-acceptance. I didn't know that the quality of the voice that I listened to inside myself would determine the entire quality of my life. It would even determine how I viewed the cosmos.

Put simply, a wildly loving inner voice gives rise to a life you wildly love.

A fearful inner voice creates a life of feeling on edge, seeing and dodging never-ending threats. Imagining it's not safe to relax. Feeling like a refugee in your own body and life.

I had always thought that the driven, critical voice within me would help me shape up and get ahead. I had no idea that voice was denying me access to my true power.

I didn't know I had a true power.

It's taken me years to realize this, but self-love is a spiritual experience.

It's the game changer of how we process every minute of our reality.

I can tell you now that learning how to fiercely champion my own life finally allowed me to trust my true desires and ease my anxiety. I could not have changed my career, written my books, created an international speaking and coaching business, thrived in a long-term relationship with a man with health challenges, and so, so much more otherwise. I have an apprehensive, obnoxious, opinionated mind, but mercifully it can be trained to focus on what helps it. So can yours.

Love lets in bigness. Love attracts creativity and opportunities. Love is a fresh frequency. It changes how the whole Universe works in your life.

There is this invisible pipeline. When we are more accepting of ourselves and our lives, we tap into the Source. We can finally hear our own inner intelligence, pure as a diamond, because we're not listening to the drone of fear, guilt, or outdated conditioning. Things begin to flow when we flow inside.

No, I'm not blissing out every day. I am not one with my cellulite, grief, or insurance premiums. I still get triggered and end up in the prison of self-judgment. But I'm light-years from where I was years ago when a therapist, a nice, gentle kumbaya type, just blurted out, "God, you're so negative."

Actually, I'm crazy happy about my life—a lot of the time now. And even about myself. And about all of us in this big human adventure. That's the path I want to share with you.

You can become your own secret weapon and shaman. You can step out of the spell. You can own the potency of your focus. Your circumstances don't have to change. Yet you can alter your entire experience.

As I champion my own life, I align with my quantum powers, my divine birthright. I trust this brilliant inner teacher, Spirit, God, the wily coyote of infinite creativity, whatever you want to call this generous energy of optimal perspective. As a result, I am being answered. Moved. *Guided.*

You may have been seeking self-improvement in different ways for a while. You are called to growth. Maybe you thought it was only about material success or having certain kinds of relationships. But I think you want more than what the world tells you that you need to be okay.

You crave a life of meaning and aliveness. You may want to know your own secret power—to fling open all the doors to your true potential. You hunger to take flight. You want what is yours. I think we all want this. We need it. But sometimes, we get confused and go buy another kitchen gadget, Big Mac, or Jaguar.

I knew I wanted to feel good and have this freedom within myself; I knew it way back then when I stumbled into my first self-improvement workshop. I knew that life had to be at least as good as the freedom to eat chicken lo mein. This is what I know now.

There's something more going on.

I am something more.

I'm going to give this ride of mine on earth everything I've got. Including love and gentleness.

Maybe you will too.

SELF-TRUST INQUIRY

What do you believe about self-love?
What are your associations with self-love?
What belief might you be willing to try on?

SELF-TRUST-ISMS

Becoming a Champion of Your Own Life

I needed to bust out of the small life that self-judgment was creating for me.

I had no clue that self-judgment was blocking the floodgates of creativity, wealth, equilibrium, and even a relationship with the juju power of the Universe.

A wildly loving inner voice gives rise to a life you wildly love.

Love is a fresh frequency. It changes how the whole Universe works in your life.

....

There is this invisible pipeline. When we are more accepting of ourselves and our lives, we tap into the Source.

....

You can become your own secret weapon and shaman . . . You can own the potency of your focus.

2

How to Stop Diluting the Brilliance Within You

THE PRACTICE: How do you hear your inner ally? **Your practice is to stop listening to any self-criticism.** Starve this voice of attention. You will never hear the voice of self-genius while you listen to the voice of self-negation. Pay attention to what you say to yourself and how it makes you feel. Let go of disempowering stories you tell yourself, and you will know exactly what to do and how to do it.

*Wisdom is avoiding all thoughts
that weaken you.*
—WAYNE DYER

*You have been criticizing yourself for years,
and it hasn't worked. Try approving of
yourself and see what happens.*
—LOUISE HAY

"You have to listen to your inner voice," I told Karen, who was trying to decide whether to move to Los Angeles or take a promotion at work. She shuddered. I honestly thought she was going to throw up. "What's going on?" I asked. She fiddled with her ring. "I don't want to listen to my inner voice," she said. "I hate my inner voice. All it does is criticize me or compare me to my older brother."

I realized we had a little problem. Actually, it's a big problem that many of us share. We hear this troll inside and think that this bitter advice is truth or our inner voice. But the opposite is true: self-criticism is the voice of your fearful inner self. Self-criticism is *not* the voice of your inner guidance. You have a loving inner voice, one of strength and thrilling awareness. In spiritual terms it's called the "still, small voice." This wise guide is waiting quietly in the background with all the power in the world, while the reactive clown in the foreground bosses you around.

It's time to retire the fearful inner voice from your life. We are going to create a new reality. And that means we are going to listen to a different advisor within. How do you hear your inner voice of love? I bet there's a thousand techniques on the internet, along with some nice spiritual activewear to better support your journey.

But the answer isn't so much what you do, but what you *stop* doing.

You stop thinking that your negativity is reality. You stop poisoning your own power. You begin to know you have a path and a guide and a way to anything that is yours. Your job is to starve the traitor, the black wolf, the ego, the voice of fear, whatever you call it, the one that steals your attention away from the counsel of your soul. Basically, it's this simple, and this challenging. **Pay attention to what you say to yourself and how it makes you feel.**

I want to share a turning-point moment in my life. It was a moment when I realized that the voice that pushed me to be "better" might just be pushing me into weakness.

Years ago, I was driving home from law school, careening down Highway 3, late at night in a stinging cold Massachusetts winter. I was furious with myself for having eaten the bag of Doritos from the clunky old vending machine. I loved Doritos. I loved their burst of flavor, a sudden flash dance in your mouth. Doritos were like a hundred fun angels coming to take the gray room of your life and paint it lime green. God forbid you're studying antitrust law while trying not to fall asleep in an oppressive library that smells like ancient sweat and dust—believe me, vending machines are sisters of mercy.

But back then I worshipped thin thighs. I wanted thin thighs. I *needed* thin thighs. My self-worth as a human being depended on them. I was anorexic and proud of it. So eating a bag of Doritos, even the mini bag, was a punishable offense. I was pretty mean to myself. This is the secret to being an excellent anorexic. You have to be mean enough to yourself that you can withstand dying of starvation at your own hand, while actually thinking you're a slouch with no control.

Okay, you may or may not have issues with food, but you might have issues with some part of your life. Pick your area. Money. Career. Relationship. It's all the same. All self-judgment blocks out the light and dilutes the epic brilliance within you. Everything opens up in your life when you stop closing your heart to yourself.

But let me get back to my Doritos incident, a moment that changed my life. I left the campus that evening feeling bad about my transgression. During this cold, dark car ride from Massachusetts to New Hampshire, my horrible inner critic ranted on and on.

You pig, I can't believe you ate those chips, the damaging voice snarled in my mind. *Did you enjoy them, huh? I hope you love your new life as a three-hundred-pound elephant.* (Note, I weighed probably all of one hundred pounds at the time.) *Don't you want to be thin? What's wrong with you? Don't you think your thighs are fat enough? Did you really need to eat those chips?*

And just like that, real life interrupted.

My small car lost traction on the road beneath me. I'd hit a patch of black ice. Speeding at sixty-five miles an hour on a well-traveled highway, I completely lost control of my vehicle. I skidded, slid, and spun into the opposing lane of oncoming traffic. It happened too fast to prevent an inevitable crash. But in a field of grace or a "lucky break," there was no traffic for just that second. No one hit me. In an alternate reality, I died. *I know it.* There was a crash and the impact proved too much for my very thin, one-hundred-pound body.

But in this reality, I pulled off the highway. I sobbed with euphoria, adrenaline, shock, and a dawning glimpse of the big picture. I was alive. I was vibrating. I couldn't stop shivering. As I tried to calm down, I felt this rush of awareness.

A few seconds earlier had almost been the last moment of my life. If that wasn't tragic enough, I would have died angry at myself. In the last minutes of my life, I would have been beating myself up for having eaten a less-than-three-ounce bag of chips. My last conscious thoughts would have been negative self-criticisms: *You are a pig. Did you really need to eat those chips? Aren't your thighs fat enough?* Off I'd go into the afterlife, with self-judgment as my send-off.

I huddled there in an altered sense of consciousness. I had one of those moments when time slowed down and I saw myself, my tiny little body in a tiny little blue Ford Pinto with bumper stickers, on a tiny little spinning planet for just the tiniest bit of time called this one precious life. I started crying harder. Heaving. Seeing my insanity with clarity.

I felt this radiant blanket of self-compassion wrap around me, quieting my heart. All I can tell you is I suddenly felt generous. It was like seeing myself from another person's point of view. I felt so bad for this young woman who was doing the best she could and who was punishing herself for having any needs at all. She was being so *indifferently cruel*. Her mind was crammed with the cutting words of a hostile terrorist or nagging fishwife. Every single day.

Years later, I remembered that night. It helped me realize that I wanted to create a radically different kind of relationship with myself. I wanted to live, breathe, and practice what the Buddhists call *maitri*, an unconditional loving kindness for oneself. I was finally exploring a path of self-awareness and, clever being that I eventually came to be, I realized I would never create a rock-star life from a nucleus of ruthlessness and self-betrayal.

I'll save you some time here. *Neither will you.*

I decided I would devote my awareness to creating a self-affirming relationship with myself. I would choose to live from love instead of fear. I would be a fierce advocate for myself. I'd encourage my growth from an authentic desire to expand, not from a shrieking need to prove myself worthy of respect. I'd already have my own respect. I'd have enough respect to listen to myself and trust my instincts, creating a life of my own right design.

I wanted to know who I could be in this life if I only fed the white wolf and cultivated a wise inner ally. Because when I do take my final breath, I want to listen to an inner advisor who sets me up for success on the next go around. *Sweetheart, I'm so proud of you. What a great ride. Can you feel the awe? Way to go, muchacha!*

Self-criticism is the language of fear. And fear—or the absence of love—is this inner narrator that we sometimes think is "being realistic." It tells us we can't trust ourselves or the deep power of our spirit. This narrator is of the old world. It's afraid of going out of business. It *is* going out of business. Fear is one of those merchants who screams at you about a sale while holding up a cracked lamp or bruised bananas. It needs to nag or shame you because it's selling something your wholeness just wouldn't buy.

The voice of fear tells you what to do in order to be safe. It never tells you that you *are* safe. It never mentions that if you stopped judging yourself, you wouldn't fall apart—you'd flourish like a hollyhock in the sun.

Sure, we're not always doing everything right. Maybe we want to stretch and grow and do things even better. That's self-awareness, not self-criticism.

Self-criticism is <u>not</u> the voice of your inner guidance.

When I am critical of myself, I'm in fear. I think I am stuck. Or broken. I think my perceptions of my circumstances are all that I will ever experience. Spiritual masters tell me I am looking at the goop of illusion. Reality is not made of stone. Reality is made of energy. Our perceptions and choices are tools we use to shape the flow. Real life is dynamic.

I am not this Wednesday. I am not this marriage or financial hiccup on a Citibank statement. I am love, electric and whole, and I can rise in any circumstance. I can uncover a strength that knows my way. There is a destiny emerging through me.

I can remind myself of how well I'm already doing. I can remember the well-being that floods my cells. I can elevate how I'm seeing my life and how I show up as a result. At any time of day, I can interrupt old neural pathways. I can change the world I live in by changing the ideas I hold about myself.

Yes, I can dance with the matrix. Love is always the energy that flips the switch.

A Course in Miracles teaches that the miracle—or love—is always here. We are here to "undo the blocks to the awareness of love's presence." That means that things are already working. There is perfection already within you: your Buddha nature or divine ember. A creative superconductor that has no limiting perceptions.

Yet we impede our wildest good because we worship ideas about ourselves that disempower us. You will never hear the voice of self-genius when you're listening to the voice of self-negation. Please take a second, if not a lifetime, and consider this: **What would it be like to listen to the continuous direction of love and positive intelligence? This is what it means to trust yourself and to create the adventure of your lifetime.**

Freedom doesn't come from pushing ourselves to be someone we're not meant to be. I wish I'd gotten *that* memo a little sooner. Freedom comes from becoming more of our authentic selves—not less. Running with our strengths. Abandoning our masks or emotional blood thinners. Belting it out in the rapture and range that we were born to sing.

When Michelangelo talked about carving his famous masterpiece *David,* he said that *David* was always already there within the marble. Michelangelo just carved away anything that wasn't truly *David*. I'm going to do the same thing with my life. I am letting go of illusions or stories that do not support my powerful self.

Self-judgment is poison. It's not discernment. It's not motivation. It's a tangle of lies. Or black flies on your pecan pie. Ironically, self-judgment holds you back from the things you want—and the things you judge yourself for not having. That's not even a catch-22. That's just a black hole. You will know the truth when you stop indulging your inner critic or any belief that cripples your life-force.

When I stop judging myself, if even for a second, I feel my heart open and I am more connected to my essential self and the presence of Spirit. I feel innocent. I feel full. I feel competent.

When I align with myself in this way, I have no doubt. I know what to do. I know who I am. I am having a totally new conversation with myself and with life.

And I can tell you, it's already been a great ride.

SELF-TRUST INQUIRY

What does your inner critic sound like?
Where does it arise most often?
What can you do to not listen to it?

SELF-TRUST-ISMS

How to Stop Diluting the Brilliance Within You

It's time to retire the fearful inner voice from your life. We are going to create a new reality.

Know you have a path and a guide and a way to anything that is yours.

Self-criticism is *not* the voice of your inner guidance. You have a loving inner voice, one of strength and thrilling awareness.

I can interrupt old neural pathways. I can change the world I live in by changing the ideas I hold about myself.

You will never hear the voice of self-genius when you're listening to the voice of self-negation.

....

Self-judgment holds you back from the things you want—and the things you judge yourself for not having.

3

I Will Not Abandon Myself
When Challenges Arise

The Practice: You are learning how not to abandon yourself or your greatest potential. Trusting yourself means holding your belief in your own path, even when things don't look perfect. **Your practice is to give yourself permission to be in process: Value cultivating a loving relationship with yourself more than you value a specific outcome.** Self-love empowers you to dare more and to not abandon things you want.

We didn't evolve for a life of all-in or one of hibernation. It's the transitions and the variations that contribute to our health, well-being, and ability to contribute.
—SETH GODIN

> *To be fully alive, fully human,*
> *and completely awake is to be continually*
> *thrown out of the nest. To live fully is to be*
> *always in no-man's-land, to experience each*
> *moment as completely new and fresh.*
> —PEMA CHÖDRÖN

I do balance poses in yoga. Lakshmi, the thirty-year-old yoga instructor, sports a demon-type tattoo on her shoulder. Let's just say the badge befits her. I swear she grins as we sweat, tremble, and try not to crash onto our mats. She says sweetly, "Falling is not failing."

As I try to stay upright in my flesh temple, maintaining equilibrium in some figure-four-type contortion, Lakshmi says, "Now bring your left knee up to your chest. Now extend your leg out." What? How can I maintain balance if she keeps adding on ridiculous cues to do *more*? *I will never be able to do this,* I yell with my inside voice. I was doing okay until she kept complicating things. I am shaking like a small dog in front of a big dog. But . . . I'm holding a version of the pose. Suddenly I understand yoga, life, and everything. I get the joke.

Ms. Demon, aka my yoga teacher, is teaching us how to embody freedom in the middle of the impossible. Finding sanity in complexity. I keep wanting to get an *A* in the pose. Or to "get there," some result that is right or makes me look perfect. I am looking at the *form* of the pose instead of the *intention* of it.

The *intention* of the practice is to learn how to stay with something and with myself when things are difficult. In a sense, the pose is irrelevant. **I am learning how to meet and sustain myself in the middle of the unbearable. I am practicing how not to abandon**

myself and my responsibility to my greatest potential. That's the gold star of gold stars. That's the super chakra happy meal.

My "balance pose" in real life is learning how to face the challenges, wonders, and shocks of everyday life and not lose touch with my belief in my path. I am practicing self-love now instead of immediate self-abandonment. Self-love helps me coach myself into buoyancy instead of the usual roadkill. This is my "balance pose" and my road to freedom.

Hold your belief in your own path one minute longer than you have before.

I used to think that getting my life in order was the most important thing I could do. I thought the form of my life *was* my life. I would hold my breath, withhold any appreciation of myself or my life until I "got there." Let me tell you, it's exhausting to wait to be happy or to be at home in your life. The fluctuations of living will always knock you off balance until you stand in the power of your self-love.

Spiritual teacher Eckhart Tolle says, "You find peace not by rearranging the circumstances of your life, but by realizing who you are at the deepest level." I'll say it like this. Can you tend to yourself, feel the sanctuary of your Essence, even when everyday life feels out of control? Your relationship with yourself and your Self affects everything you do. It affects your sense of identity, your choices, and the frequency you hold. Everything else is just a pose.

Fear pushes you to be a robot. But this I know. You don't *just* want to get things done. It's devastating to live without our own mindfulness and love. That's when negative patterns take over. You battle ghosts and regrets. Or find yourself proving yourself again like a puppet, riding the bullet train of blind ambition. But when we begin a conscious relationship with ourselves, we can finally make new decisions that rock our world.

I know what it's like to feel tired and hollow inside while chasing success. Losing yourself while thinking you're improving yourself is no fun. I want the deluxe package now—the journey of moving toward my dreams being as soul-gratifying as the imagined outcome. *I want to be in love with my life,* even when it's hard. I long to be awake, to belong to myself and to appreciate who I am and where I am with anything that's going on.

I have a feeling that my inner life is more important than my external accomplishments, and don't get me wrong, I do love me some external accomplishments. But I doubt that the meaning of life is just about pushing through things. When I leave this planet, I won't remember my huge to-do lists. I will remember the *feeling* of my hours on earth.

Here's what I'll take with me. *I will take the love I knew within.* I will take my own hand. I will bless every instance of nurturing and forgiving myself in the middle of discomfort.

I'll take in how much I *listened* to my own inner leanings or knew I was made of blue skies. I'll take in how freely I loved others and let their love touch me. And I'll walk on—in audacious, sacred friendship with an Internal Teacher who is pure magic—open to the next adventure.

DARING TO ALIGN WITH YOUR INVINCIBILITY

So forget perfection or how things appear in any given moment. What if each situation you're in is sort of perfect to help you grow your spirit in the ways that will help you most? What if you are where you're supposed to be *right now*? I know this much: transformation isn't a straight line or a race to a finish line.

Life may feel unsettling. Yet something divine and stable is going on here, the deep, quiet crux beneath it all, as though maybe there's a complex system to what seems like getting *the shift* kicked out of you.

If you saw a juggler at a street fair and he only held one plate or rubber ball, you wouldn't be that impressed. But when he throws three fine china plates up in the air and a stick of fire and whistles "Dixie," or makes a quarter or a kangaroo come out of his ear, now we're talking. Now it's interesting. Actually, it's amazing. So much wonder erupting from such a strength within. This is your assignment, too, if you choose it.

Maybe you can focus less on holding it all together and instead hold your belief in your own path one minute longer than you have before. Maybe you can maintain patience and a friendship with yourself as you grow. This is the practice of trusting yourself.

Go ahead and slip up or fall. What if it didn't matter? You are not broken ever, even when you feel broken. What if you're not fragile— but rather you've just forgotten your invincibility? You are here to grow. Dare to let things get big, instead of insisting on control. Your commitment to growth is more important than one good picture-perfect outcome. Yes, I know, you'd like the one good outcome. But you are discovering a relationship with yourself that you can trust. This is the true purpose of your inner yoga pose. This is the spectacle.

GOODBYE, PERFECTION. HELLO, PERMISSION.

I give myself permission to be *in process*. (Hey, you can join in at any time here.) Yes, take that, ego and inner "straight-A" girl. I don't want to avoid doing things because I'm afraid of making a mistake. That's too small a life. Besides, ruthless perfectionism hasn't worked out that well for me. Maybe I didn't do it perfectly.

I give myself permission to be incompetent. Inept. Lost. Terrified. And God forbid, in transition. I give myself permission to move slowly, or in rhythm with what is available. I also give myself permission to be surprised, not stuck, but morphing into someone I barely recognize but don't mind being. I give myself permission to experience a strength that is in me but somehow bigger than "me," helping me to step into a new identity. Go figure, but self-acceptance is another word for invincibility.

Maybe self-acceptance is the link that connects us with our spirit, Shakti, or a higher state of mind and equilibrium. What would it be like to discover the balancing powers of your Pure Self, the one who is untainted, undaunted, and will not ever fall, slip, or lose sight of your good? This Self can get you through anything, and will. In every situation. In every lifetime. In every back alley of your frightened mind. This quiet force is waiting to nourish your smaller self and inform it. Yet you can only experience this transformation through love and dedication to your own process.

I guess life is like one big yoga class. It's going to put us in ridiculous external postures that liberate our energy centers. Or stretch us into the impossible so that we find out just what *is* possible. It's going to ask us to leave behind what we think we know so that we can discover what a part of us has *always* known. Holy mother of meridians, we are unstoppable.

SELF-TRUST INQUIRY

Where do you need to give yourself permission to be in process?
How can you focus on cultivating a relationship with yourself
or Self, even more than you focus on other outcomes?

SELF-TRUST-ISMS

I Will Not Abandon Myself When Challenges Arise

You don't *just* want to get things done. It's devastating to live without our own mindfulness and love.

I want to be in love with my life even when it's hard.

I want the deluxe package now—the journey of moving toward my dreams being as soul-gratifying as the imagined outcome.

Hold your belief in your own path one minute longer than you have before . . . This is the practice of trusting yourself.

What if you're not fragile—but rather you've just forgotten your invincibility?

Self-acceptance is another word for invincibility.

4

You Are Here for a Reason

THE PRACTICE: You may think that being self-loving is indulgent. But listening to the voice of love within you is a matter of integrity and responsibility. You have gifts to give the world. When you doubt yourself, you deny your promise. Self-dedication isn't narcissism. It's service work. **Your practice is to own that you are here for a reason.** You are here to steward the light within you.

Child of God, you were created to do the good, the beautiful, and the holy. Do not forget this.
—*A Course in Miracles*

The person born with a talent they are meant to use will find their greatest happiness in using it.
—JOHANN WOLFGANG VON GOETHE

I am wildly fascinated with the potential of humanity. We are all mysterious powerhouses, secrets even to ourselves. I am still a little curious about my own potential too. What other tricks up my sleeve do I possess? What else awaits me in my dowry or knapsack? I know this much: **I won't really know myself until I express all of myself. Because a seed is not an apple tree. And an apple tree is not a seed.**

So this is my commitment to trusting myself. I am devoted to empowering myself for the rest of my life. I'm retiring the outdated, critical perspectives that slash my tires. I am going to love, discover, and proclaim myself. This isn't egotism. No, I am moving beyond my ego, and accepting my wholeness.

It is a life's work to cherish our own potential. This world can be a bear that tears at us with claws that shred our dreams and stamina. On top of that, most of us have landmines within, triggers that hurl us into emotional flare-ups that hold us back. When we hurt, we make smaller and demeaning choices. It seems familiar. It seems *practical.* And hell, it's popular.

That's why it's our assignment—if we choose it—to tend the powers of the invincible within us.

One day I finally decided to take up this mantle. I would emotionally and spiritually support myself or die trying. Finally, it's up to me to uncover and shape my own light. No one else will do it for me. I hate that, by the way. Then again, I'm never a fan of my own personal growth, not at the outset.

A life-affirming relationship with yourself requires focus and self-allegiance. This isn't navel-gazing. It's stargazing, feeding your own awe as you learn how to let go of every single aspect of making yourself wrong. Let me tell you there is mind-blowing strength, authority, and joy on the other side of self-blame or shame.

SELF-DEDICATION IS NOT NARCISSISM.
SELF-DEDICATION IS SERVICE WORK.

Self-dedication is stewardship. It's a rocket into the galaxy of our own capacities to heal, strengthen others, and shape the destiny of this planet. Still if all that isn't enough for you, let's just say it's your best shot of ever having inner peace.

Here's how I see it. This is my lifetime. *I am here for a reason.* This isn't a wild fantasy or the misfiring brain signals of those with stringy hair who stand on street corners with prophecies for humanity. I've been given this life to love others and unpack the gifts I have. For all I know, I carry a duffel bag of answers to prayer. I am here to give what I have, not to question, ignore, or demean it.

When I doubt myself, I deny my promise.

I muddy my creative instincts and abilities. I don't believe in blasphemy but if I did, I'd say it's blasphemy to thwart myself. **I don't think I'm put on this earth to question my self-worth—as much as to express myself for everything I'm worth.** Feeling me? I hope so.

When I'm negative about myself, even just a few measly life-sucking judgments, I can't hear the undiluted instruction of my heart or gut. Some part of me actually thinks it's useful to tell myself that I am lacking and then start tallying up the ways like a deranged accountant. This isn't just sad, it's destructive. I am closing myself off from the energy within that can fill every lack I ever thought I had.

Let's be real. Self-criticism is a wicked gift that just keeps on giving. I am harsh with others when I am harsh with myself. Unless you're enlightened or on really good drugs, I know you know those days. I can think the way my partner *breathes* is the epicenter of all my problems. Don't get me started on how he chews.

However, when I'm breaststroking in self-acceptance, I am

not challenged by others—even if they crunch on a thousand ice cubes or slurp their soup. I don't see them as demonic in any way, and not once do I think about pulling up the flowers in their garden. Self-love is the beginning of world peace, I tell you.

So this is my work now. I am taking responsibility for my life. I am taking the reins for my point of view: the voice I listen to inside myself, the stories I tell myself, my energy and vibe. I intend to use my life-force and my creativity for the good. *A Course in Miracles* teaches that inspired messengers are different from your average Western Union–type deal. They're not just delivering a message. They *are* the message. We are all a message. *We teach others what we are choosing for ourselves.*

It is a life's work to cherish our own potential.

I am asked to forgive myself, accept myself, receive myself, and express myself. I am a representative of love. I am one lantern, one way the light flies into our world. So are you.

I know you might think you already have enough on your plate without having to worry about being a messenger now. I get it. There are days when I'm lucky to have washed my hair and my "highest potential" might be getting out of bed. But at some point, if you're interested in personal development at all, you realize that everything in life goes smoother when you're coming from your best self. **It really is easier to live our highest potential than it is to deny it.**

That's why I am devoted to becoming free of self-limiting beliefs. I want to know the clarity and integrity of being undiluted. Don't you?

This kind of self-dedication isn't self-absorption. This is liberation. This is allegiance to what is true—and only what is true—the truth of who I am when I'm coming from my love and strength.

I believe in us humans. Our true nature is pretty freaking cool. We are given the chance in this lifetime to work through our misconceptions, to grow through our pain and to heal the struggles within. We can align with the best parts of ourselves, tap our storehouses of love, give our gifts, and shine like diamonds on bright white snow.

So I'm going to dare to do this and I hope you decide your life is worth this too. I will be a steward of my opportunities. I will be a dynamite concierge at this damn fine hotel. A doula of the miraculous. This is not to make me better than someone else. This is to make me better than I have been in the past. I couldn't care less about perfection. I'm a champion of the possible. I'm in it for progress, growth, and feeling great about my lifetime.

I think you owe it to yourself to realize your potential. It may even be your assignment. I know it's the source of your happiness. The truth sets us free. But you know what? It doesn't just set us free. It reverberates like a beautiful bell throughout all of time. The truth sets everyone free.

SELF-TRUST INQUIRY

Ask yourself: If I am here for a reason, what might it be? What beliefs do you hold that get in the way of your gifts?

SELF-TRUST-ISMS

You Are Here for a Reason

....

I don't think I'm put on this earth to question my self-worth as much as to express myself for everything I'm worth.

....

It is a life's work to cherish our own potential.

....

I carry a duffel bag of answers to prayer. I am here to give what I have, not to question, ignore, or demean it.

....

You have gifts to give the world. When you doubt yourself, you deny your promise.

....

Self-dedication is not narcissism. Self-dedication is service work.

....

It really is easier to live our highest potential than it is to deny it.

KICKSTARTS AND PRACTICES

Have at it. Play with these. Trust yourself. Go where you're guided . . .

Pick Three Self-Trust-isms from Part I. Journal about them. Maybe make some art. Meditate or reflect on the words that spoke to you. Discuss them with someone else. Let these chosen phrases unlock new awareness and conversation within.

1. **Recognize Your Inner Critic.** Describe this narrator as a character in a story. Listen to its catchphrases and tone. The more you become mindful of the naysayer, *without judgment,* the more you free yourself from its influence.

2. **Fill in the Blank Fifteen Times.** "If I loved myself enough, I would_____."

3. **Do an Inspired Self Dialogue Every Day this Week.** Write down what "fear" says to you. Now write to that fear from your Inspired Self, a voice of higher wisdom, strength, and love, even if it feels like you're making this up. Create a dialogue. I recommend this technique more than any other! **(There's a free, fun video guiding you with more powerful tips and my personal stories about the Inspired Self Dialogues in the Trust Yourself Mega Pack. Download this free companion collection on page 312).**

4. **What's Your Inner Yoga Pose?** What aspect of your life feels out of control? Write yourself a "Permission to be in Process" statement. Remind yourself that you want a deeper alliance with yourself, even more than "perfect" outcomes.

5. **There's a New Sheriff in Town.** Pay attention to how, when you listen to a self-compassionate voice inside yourself, you feel more connected to a sense of flow or a higher intelligence. Make your loving voice the law to follow. Swear in this authority. Post a reminder where you can see it.

6. **Mirror Mission Work.** Look into your own eyes in a mirror and speak to yourself. Own your potential and dreams. Declare that you are here for a reason and that you are accepting your assignment.

PART II

From Self-Comparison to Self-Appreciation

SHINE ON IN YOUR CRAZY GOOD LIFE

THE BLOCK: Self-Comparison
THE BREAKTHROUGH: *Self-Appreciation*

YOU GET IN YOUR OWN WAY
when you compare yourself to others.

YOU DISCOVER YOUR OWN WAY
when you appreciate yourself and your life.

~

You may not be trusting yourself because you are comparing yourself to others. Maybe you think that everyone has a better life than you. So clearly, you're making the wrong decisions. Or you were born and raised by wolves, so there's that.

*But what if you're not **seeing** your life?* It's not that you have nothing to appreciate. But you may not know *how to appreciate.* Self-trust comes from kicking your lack identity to the curb.

I invite you to step out of conditioning and uncover the unconditional joyride of your life.

The practice of appreciating yourself and the details of your life ignites a startling transformation. I think the technical term is "ripping the scales from your eyes" or "flinging open the doors of perception." This doesn't involve drugs, and it's *better* than drugs. It's being in your right mind.

How do you start to see the abundance you have and call forth even more? That's the spell we are going to cast together in this section.

5

My Focus Is a Magic Wand

THE PRACTICE: You will trust yourself more when you appreciate your life. Your happy life won't come just from acquiring possessions or the right circumstances. Joy comes from learning how to behold your world with love. Focus creates everything you think, see, and experience. **Your practice is to consciously direct your focus to see the abundance in your life right now.** There are miracles in front of you that you are not taking in. As you change your inward conversation, you will see an entirely different world.

The standard of success in life isn't the things. It isn't the money or the stuff—it is absolutely the amount of joy you feel.
—ABRAHAM HICKS

I may not need to learn anything else. Because this is my new revelation: When you love what is in front of you, everything comes to you.
—TAMA KIEVES, from a journal entry

I have this image of coming into a room where thousands of un-opened love letters accumulate. Abundance is always here in my life. But I'm not always *present*. That's the problem.

I am learning how to open those letters. Learning how to see my life with awareness. Learning how to show up as my empow-ered Self instead of the familiar, diminished version of myself.

I've always heard that "God is love." I imagined some big guy in the sky with lightning bolts and big words. Or else I imagined the Universe, some vast, spacy, hollowed-out, gaseous entity. I un-derstand things differently now. It's not just that Spirit is love. *It's that love is Spirit.* Anytime I focus on love, I am bringing that catalytic energy into the room. Everything changes with love.

True happiness isn't passive. It's our responsibility to see our lives with love. Are you willing to walk into a different life with self-awareness, sanity, and appreciation? It's mind-blowing. That's the point.

ARE YOU GETTING OR HAVING?

I'll cut to the chase here. We are not awake. We are on the take. We are in the business of getting and getting and getting. We are so busy getting that we ignore what we have. We always believe we need more. But a life of empowerment teaches us that *being is hav-ing*. When I'm fully present and receptive, I can experience more of life than all the money in the world could provide.

It's awareness that opens the door to the candy store. I am of-ten so busy doing, accomplishing, or trying to get, get, get that I am emotionally removed from my life. And when you're removed from your life, you're not *moved by anything*. You don't absorb the medicine. You don't take in the love, the fragrance, or the fullness of your own circumstances.

I'll share an example that might help you see how this goes down. I have a shabby chic, imported Chinese cabinet in my office. It's perfect. I love this thing. It has deep shelves and two large doors with half a golden circle on each side, creating a full golden circle when closed. I hide piles of papers and a riot of art supplies within. When the doors are closed, my office looks neat, and that, just so you know, is a miracle on earth.

I found this exquisite piece of furniture on sale. Hell, I wasn't even intending to look for shapeshifting, exotic furniture that day. But when my original plans changed, I wandered into this unique Asian décor and antiques shop.

Immediately I fell hard in love with this old, worn, interesting cabinet, but it was pricey. Then the shopkeeper, maybe even with a twinkle in his eye, said, "You can have it for half price. I need to clear some space for a new delivery." I felt like I was in a dream.

To my mind, this piece belonged on an interior design magazine cover. I felt like I was being allowed to date a movie star. I didn't have much money to spend at the time, but I could afford the half-price deal. I had won the lottery. Let me tell you, I felt loved. I felt awe. It was clear to me that I was being given a way when there was no way.

I swear this piece of furniture had manifested straight out of my subconscious mind. Just looking at it, I felt rich and artsy, and insecurities left my body. Let's just say if I'd seen this piece in someone else's house, I would have envied them.

Do you know what I did with this special piece of furniture after I got it into my office? I'll tell you. I ignored it. I forgot all about this miracle. Sure, I loved seeing it for a few weeks. Then it evaporated into the background of my life. It became part of the furniture, so to speak.

I had this incredible miracle sitting in my office in plain view, but I forgot my excitement, and stopped "seeing" it. I had stopped marveling at getting something I so wanted. I stopped beholding it as a love note from my enchanted life force.

I became numb because I had it already. The spirit of acquisition had been met. Yeah, it's only human.

But you know what? It's also possible to rise above unconsciousness. **You can use experiences or possessions as talismans. They can represent the power of *having* what you desire.** You can deliberately choose to focus on aspects of your life you love. Remember the power or energy that brought these people, items, or experiences into your life. You have evidence of flow and how you have already received what you have desired. It's healthy to remember that you hold this power.

Sometimes, I look around my home and find the objects I love. This practice helps me to realize that I am surrounded by things I wanted to have and have. Sometimes, when the new moon is just at the right angle in the sky, it even inspires me to clean.

WE SEE OUR STORIES MORE THAN WE SEE REALITY

Happiness isn't about what's going on. It's about *how we see* what's going on. Interpretation is the linchpin to your emotional power, the lifeblood of your life. Your stories or interpretations determine what you experience and feel. Your stories define what you see. Most important, your stories define how you see yourself.

Do you feel frustrated? Unworthy? Deprived? I guarantee you have a story going on. **You tell yourself that reality is a certain way. And then you only see that which matches your beliefs.** But you are a light and a powerhouse, and you can change the axis of your world. You can usher in a new story.

I never get what I want. Some part of me held on to this belief and chanted it like a mantra. *I never get what I want.* This was a tattoo I wore on my inner skin. My go-to default belief. *Even when I get what I want, it doesn't stick. It's there for an instant, and then it is always taken away. Now you see it, now you don't. I never get what I want,* I say. I have had this belief for years. Naturally, I have "evidence" to back up the story.

Here's an example I told therapists, coaches, boyfriends, best friends, and houseplants if they'd listen. One day when I was about ten years old, I was shopping with my mother in the department store Alexander's. I saw these red shoes in the children's shoe department. I don't remember if they were patent leather or vinyl, but I know they were red, and I longed for them in a fierce, red way.

On this one fairy-tale fantastic day, my mother granted my improbable wish. Any other day my no-frills mother would have said, "No. Let's go. You don't need those. They're too expensive. Look, these perfectly good green elf shoes are on sale." Or my mother might have said: "They're too bright. Who would wear red like that? You wouldn't like these." My mother usually treated my desires like mosquitoes; she shooed them away. However, on this day in the kingdom, I had will. It was ordained. I got those red shoes!

But then, my mother lost the department store bag that housed the new shoes. She set it down somewhere. Maybe some other mother and little girl picked it up. I don't know what happened. All I knew was she lost the bag with my ruby-red slippers. My heart was in that bag.

I never get what I want. It became a piece of my identity. The story grew in my mind. It was a parable. It was the mothership of all the satellite experiences to come after. I'd nod in recognition when someone canceled on me—*see, I never get what I want.* When a business arrangement fell through—*see, I never get what I want.* When something I desired was out of stock, *see.* You probably have the story down now.

STORIES BLOCK OUR MIRACLES

When I started opening my mind to a new reality, I realized I couldn't believe in cosmic love while I still held on to a belief that told me I would never have good in my life.

Through meditation, journaling, and personal growth work, I started questioning my ingrained beliefs, especially the ones that had me believing in a smaller world. I came to understand that I was only *choosing* to see things that validated my cheapening world view. Because there were a lot of things I wasn't really seeing, things that proved that my story wasn't true.

You see what you look for.

I wasn't taking in all the times I *did* get what I wanted. I got a book published. I got a house with a cast-iron wood stove. I got a creative best friend. I got a fast-writing pen with purple ink. I got a cool dentist who didn't lecture me about letting my Waterpik gather dust and cobwebs. It was ludicrous to think I never got what I wanted. It was delusional. *It was optional.* My ego, or the familiar self I identified with, had been opting for this perspective and fabricating misery.

So here's the thing about stories. No one is asking you to ignore the facts. But I am asking you to think about this: What does the story mean about you or someone else? It's never the facts that do us in. It's how we construe the facts. I ask all my students: What are you making this mean? It's not just what happened that continues to hurt us, *it's what we make it mean.* We create interpretations that block us from opening to love.

With my red shoes story, I made losing one pair of shoes mean I would *never* get what I wanted in life; I would *always* be a person life shorted. It's one thing to feel disappointed by an experience. But I took that feeling of disappointment and turned it into a hex or black curse, something that would continue on forever. That's the problem. That's why this story always had an extra sting and why it came up again and again. It was emotional heartburn.

That inner narrative became a blindfold that locked me into a world of my negative imagination. It was only when I started to open to the possibility that my interpretation wasn't true that I started to see other evidence. I became available to my own life.

Oh, and are you ready for the killer footnote to this story? Shortly before my mother died, I was telling her about the red shoes story, reliving the memory about how we lost the package and I never got my fantastic childhood dream. She scrunched her face in disorientation, as though maybe I had just decided to speak to her like a fax machine, screeching and clicking and waiting for her to pick up.

Then I could see a light flash behind her eyes. She did remember this semi-life-altering event in my world. Yet she remembered it differently. "You got those red shoes," she said indignantly.

"I know, but we lost the package," I reminded her. My mother looked me straight in the eyes with the sharpness of a knife. "Yes, and then I called the department store, and they found the bag. We picked it up later that night." *We found the bag?* I have no memory of this. I remembered the disappointment and deprivation. I remembered a child's lament: *I never get what I want.* I remembered my belief—more than I remembered reality.

YOU SEE WHAT YOU LOOK FOR

I put myself on the road to promote my very first book, *This Time I Dance! Creating the Work You Love.* I will always remember my first real national engagement. I spoke in a small bookstore and sold books. I remember staying at the "nice hotel," a Ramada Inn in Sacramento. I prayed to a palm tree—yes, to a palm tree, because this was California, baby, and I was a New York City girl out there in the wild west of possibility. *Please, I want more of this,* I prayed. *I want to travel and share my work. I want to be speaking and selling my books. I want this life.* It was a lot to ask of a spindly palm tree in the hot parking lot of a Ramada Inn, but I will always remember the moment. It was so pure. The desire bloomed within like a lotus.

In later years, I always noticed palm trees when I was traveling. They became one of my symbols of abundance.

Flash forward, and I am meditating on the balcony of an open, airy retreat room in Costa Rica. I am being paid to be here by a premier organization in the holistic world. It's not the first time either. I'm one of the teachers in a week-long event.

But this time, I am determined to take in the shape and fullness of goodness in my life. As I meditate, I slow down to appreciate this moment, intending to soak it in and receive it.

My inner thoughts flow something like this: *Here I am in Nosara, Costa Rica, on my balcony, my body having been dipped in the ocean at sensuous sunset. I've danced and breathed and loved in an Afro Yoga class with a sacred community of humanists, seekers, and activists. I am here. I am teaching in the Sky Mind Hall at the Blue Spirit Retreat Center, headed up by the former cofounder of the Omega Institute. Many famous teachers have taught in this exact room, with its wall of windows overlooking the expanse of ocean. I am teaching here. I feel so much love and I feel loved.*

For once, I am not focusing on what I *don't* have. I am not telling a sad tale of how I don't have as many students as some other big-name presenters, or that the bookstore didn't stock my books, or other joy-robbing thoughts which, sadly, proliferate effortlessly, if I let them. I am taking in all the good—and only the good—instead. I feel the warmth of the sun on my skin. I appreciate having time to sit here and breathe.

I bask in this moment, letting the gratitude become my anchor. I am not asking for more or less of anything. I am receiving this experience. I am focusing on being alive. The more I focus on any one grain of goodness, the more I begin to see even more nuances and dimensions. I want to weep with sudden recognition for all that I am receiving. Finally, I end my meditation.

Then I open my eyes and gaze up at the sky. And *bam,* right there is the biggest palm tree I have ever seen in my life. It's waving at me.

I burst into laughter and tears of amazement. It's such a love letter from the Universe. I am wildly amused with myself. This palm tree had been there all along. It didn't just manifest out of thin air. Yet I hadn't *seen* this tree before. I hadn't registered it. I'd been in my head. Planning the future. Grieving the past. I wasn't in the present moment, the only possible juncture where any of us can receive love.

When I consciously changed my inner conversation, I beheld a different world. I saw the abundance right in front of me all along.

SELF-TRUST INQUIRY

What do you *have,* that you once desired?
What story do you often tell yourself that might block
your abundance or appreciation of your life?

SELF-TRUST-ISMS

My Focus Is a Magic Wand

....

It's not just that Spirit is love. *It's that love is Spirit.* Anytime I focus on love, I am bringing that catalytic energy into the room.

....

True happiness isn't passive. It's our responsibility to see our lives with love.

....

A life of empowerment teaches us that *being is having.*

....

You can use experiences or possessions as talismans. They can represent the power of *having* what you desire.

....

You tell yourself that reality is a certain way. And then you only see that which matches your beliefs.

....

I realized I couldn't believe in cosmic love while I still held on to a belief that told me I would never have good in my life.

6

Burn Up the Pictures of Where You Think You Should Be

THE PRACTICE: **Your practice is to burn up the pictures of where you think you "should" be.** Dare to obey what feels right to you—instead of comparing yourself to an imaginary standard. You are on the dynamic adventure of following instincts more than conditioning. Choose love over image—and experience the freedom you have always desired.

As I let go of conditioning, I love my life unconditionally.
—TAMA KIEVES, from a journal entry

Your time is limited, so don't waste it living someone else's life.
—STEVE JOBS

Where in your life do you want to be free? Let me guess. It's a place where you're judging yourself. That's because you can't *judge* yourself and *be* yourself at the same time. Freedom means going rogue.

Burn up the pictures of where you think you should be.

A life of vision means you are following what you cannot see— but *know*. Following your heart is radical stuff. It's the commitment to follow a scent and vibration not of this world. Your life may look like less than you imagined, but do not be deceived. You do not yet know *how* to imagine. Because you're on a journey that's never been lived before. That's why self-comparison is insanity.

When you want to live your unique path, one inspired by a Source of unpredictable genius, it would be impossible to measure how you are doing by looking at the paths of others. Of course, that won't stop you from doing it. Or at least it sure didn't stop me.

I remember years ago, I was walking through the woods, under a canopy of green, chirping inwardly, feeling groovy. Then out of nowhere my mind slammed into self-judgment. It lit on a billboard I'd seen earlier advertising Newport cigarettes. A young woman my age and a hunk of a man with shocking black hair and blue diamond eyes were running through a stream, kicking up a spray of water, with blinding smiles that would make any dentist break out into an aria—and the ad read "Alive with Pleasure." Alive with pleasure? Oh my God, *the pressure*. Was I alive with pleasure? Was muzzy contentment on a Saturday afternoon good enough?

I thought I had been doing fine because I wasn't in my usual anxiety, funky, punky state of mind. Was I missing out again? Was I living a pathetic life? Oh, don't tell me, were the cool kids really kicking up their heels in streams? And just like that, I became self-conscious—which led to self-absorbed—which led to hell in a worn-out handbasket. Now my inner critic or ego was alive with pleasure, that's for damn sure.

I think we've all cast ourselves out of Eden and it's time to come back home. No offense to religion, but here's my take on things. Adam and Eve were naked and free and fine and fabulous, letting it all hang loose like grapefruits. Then they listened to a sneaky voice that made them self-conscious.

That means they probably encountered an advertisement. They saw that they did not have a Toyota RAV 4 hybrid, six-pack abs, or the best engagement on their social media campaign. It was a day of misgivings. A day of leaving behind the delight and innocence of living your own life.

We live in a world where we know too much, and yet we know so little that matters. We know what some stranger on social media ate for lunch in Bali. Still, many of us don't know what *we* want from this lifetime. We don't know how to experience our own birthright of abundance and freedom. We focus on external information and comparison. We become removed from our own lives, instead of fantastically moved by them.

TAKE BACK YOUR FREEDOM. TAKE BACK YOUR FOCUS. TAKE BACK WHERE YOU PLACE YOUR ATTENTION.

You are being hypnotized to define yourself by the standards of imprisonment: standards that make you feel less than, while promising you that you can and should have it all. I invite you to use this standard of liberation instead: *Does this thought, desire, or choice make me feel alive in this moment?* If not, it's a lie. It's a veil over the truth. **The truth is that freedom comes from feeling connected to our essence, strength, and love—more than it comes from our circumstances.**

I remember a time when I almost allowed self-consciousness to keep me from experiencing one of my life purposes, which is creating sacred, life-affirming experiences for others. I wanted to throw a potluck party for the students in my local *A Course in Miracles* community, but I was nervous about it. I kept thinking that as a national author and expert success coach my home should look a certain way, you know, like something from a movie or glossy magazine.

I was stuck in image-land. My ego insisted that I should have a home that looked sleek and self-secure, like women with long legs, stark bangs, and French accents who could star in James Bond movies. My house was more Bridget Jones: endearing, but no photo shoots happening here. I didn't have a chef's kitchen the size of a barn with a Bosch stove and recessed lighting in my cabinets. My ego lashed out at me and told me I was a total fake of a success, because my "extraordinary life" was ordinary.

I will not live my life for what it looks like
but for what it feels like.

I surveyed my backyard, where we would gather for part of the time. My worn wood fence looked tired, like maybe it was going through menopause. The latest weeds and vines were having themselves a bacchanalian rumpus, defying any implication of landscape design. I said to my partner, Paul, "Is this how a successful author lives?" He laughed and said, "Yes, this is *exactly* how this successful author lives. You've got other priorities. You are speaking in other cities, coaching, writing, moving your message into the world." This is why I love this guy. I laughed out loud as I looked at a thatch of dandelions. "God, am I successful," I said.

Talking to another friend about having the party, she said, "No one needs another pedestal-perfect expert or untouchable guru." I felt relieved. I really didn't want to have to buy a chateau with a heliport just so I could have an impromptu gathering. But the crappy voice inside my head wouldn't relent. *This is where the national author lives,* it taunted.

I love my house. My house is over a hundred years old, sweet, and in a wonderful urban neighborhood in Denver. I bought it with money I made from doing only the work I love. My house has an exposed brick wall and an old wood stove that I cherish. But some days this is not my wildest dream house. Yet it's a self-betrayal to allow myself to slide into awkward embarrassment.

For years, I have chosen to put more of my money and energy into becoming a writer and uncovering the depth of my calling. I have deliberately chosen to live below my means. I craved freedom more than I wanted reconstruction projects. It's just that I sometimes forget all of that and think I should be impressing people.

After talking with my friend, I focused on what was right about my life. Here's what made me feel all glowy rich. While I don't drive the latest Mercedez Benz or a have formal dining room with ninety-foot ceilings, I've tasted passion and life on my own terms. Hell, a few mythical golden eagles might even have circled above me, digging my freedom. You can't buy that on Rodeo Drive, no matter how much money you spend.

Comparison to others—or even to an imagined benchmark of myself—takes me out of my right equation. I am not here to be "the national author," the image of whatever she is supposed to be. I am here to walk my path and discover the evolution of my truth.

I follow the Self that instructs me, because truth be told, I don't know the real way to happiness on my own. I am learning how to step out of my old ideas of good and bad, big and small, success and failure, and follow the heat of instinct. There is more beauty and possibility in this life. Finally, I am willing to step out of conditioning—and uncover an unconditional love for my own legendary, kickass path.

Lao Tzu said, "He who defines himself cannot know himself." This is hard for us image freaks or those who know which hoop you need to jump through to get that societally given *A*. But there is something that feels better than the "right image." *Your right life* feels better than the right image.

Your right life comes from trusting yourself. Trusting yourself means getting out of your measuring mind—and opening your heart to *what is*. You have no idea *what is* until you let go of judgment and start listening to your guidance. The love you seek is in your life, not in your imagined life.

Self-trust is appreciating yourself like you have never done before. You realize you're after a different kind of *A*. You want the full monty . . . the kind of connection to yourself that does not change, even when circumstances do.

This has been my hugest shift. **I will not live my life for what it looks like, but for what it *feels* like.** I don't want to miss a moment of my life because I'm underwater in self-comparison. Believe me, I've missed *a lot* of moments this way. Can you relate? I am committed to showing up for my life . . . and even my agitated comparing self—with all the love I can. I am not my circumstances, and neither are you. I am the free soul who creates the meaning of the experience I'm in. I am the one who is sometimes available enough to come from an open heart instead of fear of criticism.

Thank goodness I decided to have people over that night years ago, even without a remodeled kitchen or a manservant or a panoramic ocean view with scheduled whale sightings. Did I mention I live in Denver?

The night I threw the party, there was so much crazy love. People came. They brought their children, their dogs, their worn guitars, their spinach casseroles, double Dutch chocolate gluten-free cake, and their life's dilemmas and insights. There were immediate intimate conversations, even among strangers; laughter; tears; and not much small talk. I loved watching people come home to themselves, in my sweet home with weeds in the backyard.

A wave of deep peace and connection permeated this spontaneous evening. Something mystical had happened. *I am a billionaire of soul,* I thought afterward. I will die in peace. You can't measure the return on investment of this kind of success. I didn't get on *Good Morning America,* my company didn't do an IPO, and I don't think I even understand what that is. But my shoulders were loose, my blood warm. I had light in my eyes. I felt very, very rich and lucky.

My friend Ann, who is a bit of a shaman and a life coach and who will pull anything out of her hat that helps, started talking to me about Jesus—the rebel, not the icon. She said Jesus didn't make distinctions about what was big success and what was small. He didn't just attend the A-list parties. He entered all of life wherever it met him.

He hung out with the outcasts who didn't drive new chariots even when he had enough personal power to pig out at Cold Stone Creamery every day without gaining a pound, a zit, or a heart condition. Mind you, I'm paraphrasing. "The dude was free," she said. We both sighed with admiration. I think the dude would have loved my potluck.

I'm not saying you shouldn't have possessions, ambitions, or goals.

Your freedom might come by living bigger and getting that BMW or eight-foot dining room table. Your true expression might require lavish wealth or fame. Yet you might be thinking that you need to be modest or that you don't deserve it. Trusting ourselves means we allow ourselves to have the life experiences that most support our souls. We don't judge what those experiences are.

You might be drawn to live in a yurt. Or you might let yourself buy an even bigger yacht. It's not the lifestyle that matters. What matters is why you're doing what you're doing: Is it conditioning or *guidance*? Are you following the love within you? Or are you listening to the opinions of others—even though they don't hear the same inner voice that you do?

Here's the main thing, you fabulous seeker. Whatever life you're in, do not make yourself wrong. Please don't judge your worth based on how you imagine that things might look to others. May you never hold back your love—ever—because of what you think you don't have.

Sure, you may still want other things. In fact, you may always discover and refine desires. You're in process. But you can be whole *and* in process at the same time. Take it from me, one former image-conscious crazy person who is learning to enjoy her life because she has finally figured out that this is a once-in-a-lifetime opportunity. This is my freedom stance and maybe it speaks to you: **I will love the life I have—while I continue to create even more of the life I desire.**

Hell, I may even kick up some streams in my life and be alive with pleasure.

SELF-TRUST INQUIRY

Where do you make yourself feel bad about how
your life looks?
Do you have an image of what your life is "supposed" to
look like that gets in the way of your life's adventure?

SELF-TRUST-ISMS

Burn Up the Pictures of Where You Think You Should Be

....

You're on a journey that's never been lived before ... self-comparison is insanity.

....

Take back your freedom. Take back your focus. Take back where you place your attention.

....

You have no idea *what is* until you let go of judgment and start listening to your guidance.

....

The love you seek is in your life, not in your imagined life.

....

I will not live my life for what it looks like, but for what it *feels* like.

....

May you never hold back your love—ever—because of what you think you don't have.

7

Do You Lack Support?
Or Do You Support Lack?

THE PRACTICE: You may have a secret lack identity. This part of you assumes that everyone else has more support than you: more money, connections, or love. Your journey requires you to let go of the idea that you are without resources. You do not lack support. You support lack—with your faulty perspective. Break free from the lie. **Your practice is to pay attention to the countless sources of support you have already experienced.**

For he shall give his angels charge over thee,
to keep thee in all thy ways.
—PSALM 91:11

You are not separate from the whole.
You are one with the sun, the earth, the air.
—ECKHART TOLLE

For a very long time, I secretly felt like I didn't have support in my life. I'd cringe when I watched the Grammys or Oscars. "I want to thank my mother who always believed in me." Or sob, sob, "I want to thank my husband who financed my dreams." *I want to thank . . . myself . . . for not throwing up right now,* I'd think.

Maybe you feel like other people get to live grand, well-oiled lives, but that you don't. Many of us house this secret lack identity within us.

Yet what if your secret lack identity is just a bad snake charmer that diverts you from experiencing your shining, rich, complex life? You can make choices right now that will change your entire experience.

I'd like to share with you one way I began to step into a world of support and continuous grace, despite my jealous self. It's one of those practices that can seem simple and yet it can fling open the saloon doors into an entirely new world.

Years ago, I had finished leading a retreat, and it had gone very well. But after my professionalism receded, my personal life grabbed me by the throat with a cry for help. There were unsettling changes going on in my world.

My best friend who also helped me in my business was very sick and was going in for a super scary diagnosis. My business felt like an old, dilapidated bus heaving up mountains or speeding down and around dirt curves and I was driving this bus alone, only I had no idea how to drive.

At night in bed, I couldn't sleep. I felt as though I was alone in this life under a vast sky while everyone else had families to support them, knitting groups or communes or something.

During my retreat, I'd been holding my feelings of overwhelm and that feeling of terrible isolation at bay. At my lowest point, I even started envying my students, which is wacko even for me.

They had support *like the support I was giving them* in this retreat. I wanted support like that.

That's when I knew the feeling of being on my own with everything was destroying me and I needed to calm down, and hell, I was at a retreat center. I decided to get a massage, which I never do. I was reaching out for someone to take care of me, if only for an hour.

"I feel like an orphan in the world sometimes," I told Ella, the witchy-holy-woman-French-masseuse at the retreat center. "I don't have a close family like other people, or a posse of friends like in *Sex and the City*." My new captive best friend was small but strong. She kneaded the abacus beads and bits of concrete in my shoulders.

The brochure said she did massage, energy work, ancestral work, and other gobbledygook, a term my cynical mind uses preemptively and generously. I chose her because she was the only one available at the hour I could do it. *Yeah, like that was an accident.*

Ella was as thin as one of the strands of her stringy, stripy gray hair, yet she was formidable. She was a puma who could take down a rhinoceros or a skyscraper. I took in the thought that *she has my back*. Literally.

She listened, then interrupted, "Oh, so you have no support in life?" Then she laughed, as though I were the most amusing creature she'd ever met. The woman had lived in Southern California for a decade, so that was saying a lot.

"No support?" she said again. "Did you grow the yellow squash or pick the mangoes for your salad at the retreat center today? Did you filter the water you drank? Build the roads that led here?" she went on in her bewitch-y French accent.

"We are all supporting you. The world is interconnected. No one is alone. No one is untouched." As she talked, I suddenly had a feeling that she was speaking a spell of truth, one that started to awaken trust. I could feel this warm kindness seep into my being.

The Universe became one beaming energy being, one breathing

entity, and all of it pulsed with love. I saw how the world was teeming with contribution and generosity, despite so many examples of things that seemed wrong. That small gray-haired gnome turned my desperation into faith. Then again, it could have just been one hell of a massage.

MESSENGERS AND BENEFACTORS

I chose to see that masseuse as a messenger in my life. She was what I have learned to call a benefactor.

She was just one of the myriad ways my Spirit has bolstered and cradled me when I needed it. I had no idea that she was someone who would help me. I had no idea that I even needed the kind of support she offered.

I had always been a bit literal, thinking support had to be someone who wrote you a check. Or wiped your chin and told you, "You are made of fairy dust, and I will always be here." As I've opened up to experiencing a spiritual adventure in this lifetime, I have loosened my parameters, my ideas about who is supposed to support me, or how support is meant to arrive.

I've even expanded my definition of family and kinship: they don't have to be related to me. They don't have to support me forever or even beyond one singular instance. I might not know them yet. I may not recognize the support I received until later. There are thousands who I can connect to: beautiful souls, alive and beyond, who always want the best for me.

In his book *Buddha Is as Buddha Does*, Lama Surya Das shares a Buddhist discipline of holding your benefactors in your awareness. This practice is to remember those who have helped you cultivate your open heart. He shares an example of a gruff mechanic in a small town who fixed his car on credit when he didn't have the funds. And Nelson Mandela, who supported generations by being an example of the magnificence of forgiveness.

When I looked for the benefactors in my life, my memories sprang alive. The more I looked, the more I saw: my second-grade teacher who told me it was okay when I started sobbing because I couldn't draw a map. Some pale clerk who gave me a free cup of coffee at a 7-Eleven. The rain that watered my garden. The optometrist who fixed my purple glass frames gratis when my dog chewed them up.

Then there was Helen Schucman, the professor of medical psychology at Columbia University who dared to scribe *A Course in Miracles,* which helped me, and millions of others, to move beyond our fears. My first client who said I was the best thing that had ever happened to her. A stranger on her porch who smiled at me just when I was thinking I didn't belong in the world.

Or the crispy, tanned grandmother who was picking up litter on the beach on Christmas Day in Encinitas, California. She was Santa Claus in shorts, only her satchel was stuffed with garbage. I felt a flicker of hope when I saw her. There are people everywhere who are working to make a difference and we don't even know about them. This beach-loving environmentalist was supporting me—and the world—in bare feet without saying a word.

> *You are not supporting yourself when*
> *you tell yourself you are not supported.*

I have gotten what I needed from authors, artists, and visionaries I have never met. Or even from a driver who slowed down and didn't hit me and screw up a particularly useful organ for the rest of my life. Or a rotten boyfriend who made me realize I really did need to value myself more.

I am not separate and alone. I am living in a responsive, dynamic Universe, a web of energy. And I have a voice of a loving internal teacher that writes to me in my journal, *I have always sent you what you needed. I always will.*

DO YOU LACK SUPPORT—
OR DO YOU SUPPORT LACK?

Maybe you don't have a trust fund like the rest of us, who are all rolling around in ease and fluidity. Maybe you don't have connections in Hollywood or at the school you want your child to attend. Maybe you don't have a body that can run a marathon. Maybe you grew up without any advantages and not even one lousy beach house on Nantucket.

But here's what you do have—when you're not in fear. You have access to a quiet depth of knowing within you, a sea of healing. You have your God or sexy higher wisdom—something "other" than your limited understanding. These days, we even have the laws of quantum physics that calibrate how energy changes as we change our focus. The grace you experience in your life is up to you.

Let's face it, we're hooked up even when we don't realize and activate it. What if we lived our lives trusting this deeper and higher connection? Maybe you've heard a radio commercial for the Shane Company, a jewelry store that specializes in engagement rings. The commercial tells listeners not to worry about prices, because "Now you have a friend in the diamond business." One day I smile to myself, and I say out loud, "Now you have a friend in the creating-your-optimal-life business."

It felt fun to imagine that I had an "in" because I knew the

CEO. In fact, I was a personal favorite. At any time if I looked out of the corner of my eye, I'd catch her winking at me and grinning. Hey, I'm convinced this is truer than not, though maybe the CEO is a bit amorphous and vast as space and shows up as both particle and wave. Still, I've got a connection. So do you.

A friend of mine reminds me, "With Spirit, all things are possible." I think she may have New Aged–up a Bible quote, but it does the trick for me. It reminds me that I am not alone and stuck with the thin chances my smaller self sees. I can plug into my creativity, my moxie, my faith, and the dimension-bending powers of that great Something Else. I am not powerless or stuck in self-judgment purgatory.

Maybe you know this magic. When I returned to "right mindedness," I felt connected to an awareness and grace inside myself. The world started to mirror hopeful things. I met someone significant. A new client called. That thing called synchronicity found its swing.

Eventually I lost this sense of internal support again, almost always because I slipped into my secret lack identity by comparing myself to someone else or to some ideal in my mind. I focused on what I thought I didn't have. I took the road that leads to the house of horrors, a path that is so well traveled it walks itself and packs a lunch.

Neuroscientists tell us that habitual thinking creates grooves in the brain. That's why some of our thoughts feel so familiar and automatic. Unfortunately, we can mistake the feeling of "familiar" for "true."

Theodore Roosevelt nailed it when he said, "Comparison is the thief of joy." Yet it's worse than that. Comparison robs your luminous identity. **You forget who you really are when you start looking at who you are not.**

THE FIRST WAY TO FIND SUPPORT: LET GO OF IDEAS THAT DO NOT SUPPORT YOU

Let go of the idea or image of you being stuck or broken or un-loved. It's a lie, a trance we all fall into. Stand up for your life. Become an ally of your own abundance. Guard your perspective because your perspective will become your world.

No matter what you're facing right now, ask yourself, where am I not supporting myself? Here's a hint: **You are not supporting yourself when you tell yourself you are not supported.**

Intensify your well-being. Train yourself to see and experience support. Your life makes sense, even when things feel hard. There's a transcendental clarity and design at work. Life is often savage and beautiful at the same time, but always there is an undercurrent as steady as your breath.

Open your eyes. **Your benefactors, messengers, and camouflaged angels surround you. The more you choose to see them, the more of them you will see.** When you witness how much you are reinforced in life, it changes what you imagine you can have.

Who would you be if you knew you were supported all the way? I dare you to find out.

SELF-TRUST INQUIRY

Who have been the benefactors in your life?
Who is a benefactor right now?

SELF-TRUST-ISMS

Do You Lack Support? Or Do You Support Lack?

....

You do not lack support. You support lack—with your faulty perspective.

....

I felt as though I were alone in this life under a vast sky while everyone else had families to support them, knitting groups or communes or something.

....

You forget who you really are when you start looking at who you are not.

....

You are not supporting yourself when you tell yourself you are not supported.

....

Your benefactors, messengers, and camouflaged angels surround you. The more you choose to see them, the more of them you will see.

....

When you witness how much you are reinforced in life, it changes what you imagine you can have.

8

There Is No Better Life Than Yours

THE PRACTICE: You may be making yourself wrong for feeling as though you are not in a solid life. But everyone is in a life of flux. Appreciate your moments now. There is no better life than yours. The path of trusting yourself deeply is cultivating self-allegiance through ebbs and flows. **Your practice is to seize your sparks of light and focus on what is working.** This will give you direction and strength even when things change.

Nothing in the world is permanent, and we're foolish when we ask anything to last, but surely we're still more foolish not to take delight in it while we have it.
—W. SOMERSET MAUGHAM

Rejoicing in ordinary things is not sentimental or trite. It actually takes guts. Each time we drop our complaints and allow everyday good fortune to inspire us, we enter the warrior's world.
—PEMA CHÖDRÖN

Have you ever thought that everyone else has a perfect life and that maybe if you could figure it out, you'd finally slide into an idyllic life that never fluctuates? Maybe you're making yourself wrong for, say, the human condition.

We are all living lives of impermanence. We are all in flux. This is more reason than ever to appreciate every detail you love about your life. Appreciation makes you stronger. The search for an illusion makes you miss the love in front of you.

It was my last day in New York City. I was leaving Central Park to catch a Southwest plane back to Denver. Of course, on the last day of my trip, it wasn't biting, make-you-want-to-scream-out-loud-and-confess-to-sins-you-didn't-even-commit cold. It was spring, *suddenly spring,* suddenly this warmth that could make you forgive anything, even yourself. I was in Central Park with horses with purple plume feathers clip-clopping by, pulling carriages of new lovers and tourists from Japan.

I longed to hold on to the feeling, the feeling of such goodness, like your first great kiss or getting a call back from an audition. Just at that moment, I saw the Bubble Maker. He was a scruffy man in his thirties sporting a knapsack and red pants, and he was dipping this huge dipper into liquid rainbow gloppy bubble goo and spreading it, making a long, big, iridescent glob of magic.

What a great picture, I thought. Yet every time I tried to snap a photo, he moved. I missed the moment. I snapped a blur. This was a great metaphor for my life. I'm no fool. I know a message when I see one.

I realized then that **I am always trying to turn the miraculous into permanence.** I don't want to go through ebbs and flows or a stupid incubation or "process."

I don't want slow times in my business. Or a friend's spouse suddenly killed by a drunken driver. Political unrest. A rangy mind. I don't want to be in between things.

I want bling. I want peak experiences. I want high tide all the damn time. I want my positive circumstances to stay exactly the same. I want to have enough money so that I can buy bubbles that last a lifetime. I dread the return to insecurity. I just want to be "there" in some kind of ironclad life.

Of course, this is not exactly how the ride of life works.

Though it is what television commercials promise, if I buy the right SUV or medication. I'm led to believe I can have it. In fact, others have perfect lives all the time. That's what my crazy, unsupervised brain tells me, even while I know cancer, accidents, and misfortune strike the rich and thin too. But no, my mind tells me, they are partying in Ibiza, making trillions of dollars, and dominating world stages. They have happy marriages crammed with Hallmark Christmases and friends at ski chalets.

Get this: they have spouses who are more caring than your therapist, your acupuncturist, and your favorite barista combined. Their children weep with gratitude for them and never take opioids. *I have the best mom in the whole world, she's my best friend,* they say with gooey eyes. My mind can torment me until the day is long. This is why I'm ferociously dedicated to a conscious life and spiritual awareness.

Unrealistic fantasies deny us the power of our own unparalleled lives. Because the tangy magic of life is in experiencing joy and hope, while also opening to grief, radical acceptance, and growth when shifts occur. There is only this option, even if you whine or hunt for a loophole. We're all on one hell of a ride. There isn't anyone, anywhere, who goes through life without turbulence and bruises.

I've always been moved by this quote from Scottish author Ian Maclaren: "Be kind, for everyone you meet is fighting a hard battle." Yes, even your coworker. Yes, even the people in commercials or digital nomads trekking the globe. We're all on a spiritual journey whether we call it that or not. We all battle injustice, fear, and private hobgoblins. Yet we have the opportunity to become remarkable through love—to choose self-renewing courage over any diminishment. The world can't do this for us. But we can do this for the world.

It takes practice to remember that I *want* this wild ride, and that illusions of perfection only distract me. At times, I just can't help but smile with buckets of self-compassion for all my needy, grabby instincts. I am so charmingly misdirected.

Of course, there is nothing *wrong* with wanting unending joy. It's just that this distraction robs my joy.

You know how it feels when you're grasping for something and then it seems further away? This is the opposite of receiving your life. The Buddhists talk about how we create pain for ourselves by becoming attached to results. We resist the unfamiliar. We push away what we perceive as obstacles, loneliness, or the lack of love. We separate from our own lives. We separate from ourselves.

I'm still not always sure how to embrace it all: certain disappointments, broken promises, jealousy, aging, fear of the unknown, and then the ridiculously cruel things like Netflix canceling my favorite series. But I do know that it's about being more compassionate with myself and trusting my life. It's about not beating myself up for where I am but opening to curiosity or even mercy. Mercy goes a long way. A sacred, loving intelligence only wraps its aura around me when I quiet the self-attacking harpy pecking at my head. I guess even cosmic forces don't want to get next to that racket.

You may not yet be able to see the good in a particular circumstance, but you can steady yourself as you face discomfort. Self-compassion warms you like the sun. This is a great start. This may even be the finish line.

LET GO OF GRASPING. DO PURSUE JOY.

Maybe I can't have joy 24/7 like 7-Eleven Twinkies. Of course, that doesn't mean I don't pursue joy. My heart's desires create expansiveness. I am designed to follow the code within me and express my love. I'm here to seize the light that is available—and its presence reminds me of who I really am.

I've read that in the Kabbalah, the Jewish mystical text, there is the instruction to look for *the sparks in the world,* because sparks of holiness are woven into the fabric. I teach my students and clients to notice what is already working in their lives and in the world. This focus trains us to be buoyant. We prioritize what we want to see. You wouldn't believe how effective this is once you start to use it.

I also ask my students to stop looking for guarantees, or a direction or happiness that will never shift. No one likes to hear this, though I think a secret part of them feels relief. The truth about change makes them nimble and responsive to their instincts. Now they are available to even *more* good in their lives because they no longer clutch at just one definition or expression of happiness.

> *You can't take from me*
> *the dances that I've danced.*

My mother once told me, "A happy life is about the moments." My mother who had not traveled much in life or gone to fancy places, who saved worn matchbooks from Italian restaurants or places I'd taken her when she'd visited Colorado. She crushed a wildflower into her favorite romance novel and collected pretty notecards. "I ate the best fresh cherries," she'd say, "and they were on sale."

My mother was no mystic or rabbi. She'd never watched *The Secret* and she'd never heard of Rumi. But in her way, she seized some sparks in the world. She took in her holy moments. They gave her strength.

I know the Bubble Maker probably went home to his small, crammed studio apartment filled with books and a clanking radiator. Maybe it's loneliness that made him take the uptown 1 train to Central Park and spread bubbles. At home, he folded his red pants up or threw them in a pile. He ate pizza or hummus or takeout Chinese. Maybe he journaled some wayward thoughts. Because even the man who makes the magic is sometimes longing for magic.

I am grateful to him for sharing a spark of joy—and for all who follow inspiration. The Bubble Maker winged color and light and delight into the spring breeze, and those bubbles are now embedded in some tourist's memories, a child's fantasy, an old man's amusement. Maybe you too will pursue your inspiration and not worry about where it goes. It's never a waste of time to follow your excitement or share your sparks of holiness.

It turns out that while beauty and hope are not permanent, they are eternal. The form passes. The essence remains. No act of love is ever lost.

Appreciate your moments now. This is your adventure. There is no better life than yours. **When we start to take in the love or beauty of our lives, we experience a sense of security we thought we would find only in the right job, the right spouse, or the right life.** I had a Cuban friend tell me long ago a saying he translated into English like this: "You can't take from me the dances that I've danced." I've never forgotten his wisdom. I've never heard of a better definition of security or abundance.

SELF-TRUST INQUIRY

Where are you trying to make something permanent?
What is working in your life right now?
What are some sparks of light you can seize or share?

SELF-TRUST-ISMS

There Is No Better Life than Yours

We are all living lives of impermanence . . . this is more reason than ever to appreciate every detail you love about your life.

Appreciation makes you stronger. The search for an illusion makes you miss the love in front of you.

Of course, there is nothing *wrong* with wanting unending joy. It's just that this distraction robs my joy.

It's never a waste of time to follow your excitement or share your sparks of holiness.

When we start to take in the love or beauty of our lives, we experience a sense of security we thought we would find only in the right job, the right spouse, or the right life.

You can't take from me the dances that I've danced.

KICKSTARTS AND PRACTICES

Have at it. Play with these. Trust yourself. Go where you're guided . . .

Pick Three Self-Trust-isms from Part II. Journal about them. Maybe make some art. Meditate or reflect on the words that spoke to you. Discuss them with someone else. Let these chosen phrases unlock a new awareness and conversation within.

1. **Create a Daily Win List for a Week.** Each day, write five wins. Capture positive achievements, including emotional accomplishments, such as times you chose to be self-compassionate. Include moments of magic, synchronicity, or being helped.
2. **Get "There" Now.** If you were in your ideal life, what would you be doing? Get specific. Do one thing now. Can't go to Paris? Maybe you could go to a French sidewalk café, or watch French films?
3. **Your Envy-Worthy Résumé.** Write your life résumé. Plump up all your accomplishments. Also list your blessings. The love you have in many forms. The things "in the works." Your superpowers. Go lavish, baby. Don't be modest.
4. **Tell Your Stellar New Story.** Take a negative story you have about yourself or your life and write a fun, positive new story. *Feel the feeling of this.* Start noticing the details of your life that match this story.

5. **List Your Talismans.** Look at the items in your home or life that represent things you wanted—and now have. Include experiences too. Can you showcase any of these talismans? Practice experiencing *the feeling of having what you desire.*

6. **Your Life-Changing Mantra.** Say this to yourself as often as possible: "I do not want to be anywhere else." This is better than Abra Cadabra!

PART III

From Self-Doubt to Self-Trust

FINDING INSPIRED ANSWERS

THE BLOCK: Self-Doubt

THE BREAKTHROUGH: *Self-Trust*

YOU GET IN YOUR OWN WAY
when you doubt yourself.

YOU DISCOVER YOUR OWN WAY
when you trust yourself.

———❧———

You may not trust yourself because you doubt the desires and hunches that don't make sense to the historic you. But will you listen to who you are called to become now?

Your linear mind fights the intuitive or new. It says: You are naive and unrealistic. Why can't you be practical? It's not like you're toiling away in a salt mine in Siberia. You want the fantastical. No one normal is waiting for instruction from invisible forces.

But what if you are called to grow beyond what you have known before?

The path of self-trust is a process. Your way is off the map, but also off the charts. The rules are different now. Each moment has an instruction. Something alive is happening. You are having a love affair with your Inspired Self. This is life on another level. You know you're on your path.

In this section, we look at how to discover your true answers and yourself.

9

Follow Your Breadcrumbs

THE PRACTICE: Happiness is dynamic. You are in a sacred process. This is not about looking for "the answer" or a plan. You are required to follow your breadcrumbs, the desires of each moment—even when they don't make sense to you. Your mind may be trying to figure things out, but this is a path of *feeling* things out. **Your practice is to follow the desires or inclinations that give you energy.**

I start making friendship bracelets for fun.
And then I kill everything by googling how
much money craft artists make.
—A STUDENT FROM MY WORKSHOP

Seize your wild want, not that freeze-dried
politically correct mild want . . .
Only the real dream has the power.
—TAMA KIEVES, from *This Time I Dance!*

A LIFE OF LOSING AND FINDING YOURSELF

The thing about finding your way is this. There's no owner's manual or cheat sheet. No tour guide or souvenir shop. This is not a trip for tourists. This is the trip of travelers. Your feet crunch on the ground and you must listen to your own heartbeat. There is a footpath to freedom that only you can find.

When it comes to your true path, no one else can tell you where you belong. It's okay to stumble or lose your way. Go ahead and probe, make mistakes, step on snakes, or do a few takes of the scene that might not even get into the movie. Because you will get this right. *You will find what's yours already.*

It's the process that gives you clarity.

Yes, there it is. That dreaded word: process. An authentic life isn't as simple as finding the right track—and then you're set for life. This will be an adventure of *continuously* finding yourself and your next steps through presence and focus. You are worth this level of attentiveness.

Of course, I thought that finding my path would be a one-time thing. I thought it would be like riding an escalator at the mall, humming to Muzak, once you identified that one right place to stand.

But no. Trusting myself has been a pattern of losing and finding my way. It can seem like I have the worst GPS system in the world, but actually, I'm realizing I have seriously sensitive equipment. You do too. Built-in, factory issued.

Maybe you think that you shouldn't have to keep searching. Or that a time of disconnection is the telltale sign that you are—to put it nicely—*screwed.*

Yet I think we "lose the signal" as a reminder to pay attention. We learn the habit of listening to ourselves more deeply. We learn to sort through experiences and discern fresh clarities that guide us even more. If we didn't lose our connection, let's face it, some of us—and I'm not naming names here—might just call it good and start zoning out on this stardust journey. That defeats the system of *staying awake* to your true path.

Happiness is dynamic. You are forever growing into who you are meant to be. You want to stay up to date with who you are now. Your identity is an algorithm, not a single label on a résumé. The world of stimulus is perpetually changing. So you will lose your way. It's part of finding your way.

BESIDES, YOUR CALLING KNOWS THE WAY

Years ago, I left the identity of being a lawyer to find my calling, or a life that made sense to me. Ever since that time, I have felt as though I'm making my path up as I go along. On the one hand it has felt makeshift, cobbled together from breadcrumbs, hunches, and something like an inner signal that stutters in Morse code with a lisp.

> *My desires are holy. I know that*
> *because they give me energy.*

I could look at my choices through the eyes of my linear mind, and I'd see them as simple-minded as rubbing two sticks together or following a lemony butterfly. But when I look back, I see my journey has been as sound as stone. Maybe even set in stone. I can't help but feel as though this life has been waiting for me all along.

I didn't have a plan. Yet I did seem to have a trajectory.

I didn't know what I was doing. I still don't know exactly what I'm doing. There's nothing black-and-white about this. I am discovering and expressing all my true colors.

Because here's the thing. When a calling calls you, the calling knows what it's doing. (Yes, *you* have a calling.) Your calling is the expression of your spirit. Your calling is the life that is calling to you now, and this life has its own voice. That's why we do not lead. *We are led.* We receive direction from within, even when it's a direction that doesn't seem to make sense to us—yet.

For example, you may think you're not "doing" anything. But maybe you are feeling the feelings that must be felt before you can move on. You may be grieving. Or punching walls. Or working with an anxiety that has always held you back.

These are fierce achievements. Such heroic acts of self-love. Many of us need to detox from an old life of self-abuse or self-denial. There is no galloping into full potential until we repair our heart's broken bones. We are learning how to heal and reclaim our strength and faith. What we learn in the middle will carry us to the finish line.

My path has felt like an unmarked dirt path, but I have felt marked as I walk it. I have felt like something alive was happening, even if I couldn't control or predict it. I have felt spottily guided at times. But really this could be because I immediately tried to beat down any idea that didn't match a preferred image of myself. Yet through everything I've walked through, and there's been a lot, something always worked. *Something always works.*

Something will work for you. Listen to yourself. Trust yourself. Honor the language that you and your guidance speak to each other. This is the invitation of your lifetime. Will you listen to your undiminished fire or spirit? Or will you live by what other people think? Or what your fear tells you is the "right way" of doing things, even though it differs from how you naturally feel called?

It's easy to let the media, the newest trend, the school system, our family, or the muggles of the Harry Potter world define our unnameable reality. You might cling to the opinion of someone else, even though it feels horrible, which tells you something right there.

It takes so much courage to remember that there is no static reality. The world is what you make of it. This is your moment. This is your journey. And you are called to follow the intuitive intelligence within and discover the expression, the bounty, and embodiment that is yours and only yours.

This is the price of freedom. You think for yourself. You feel your guidance. You trust your trip.

FOLLOW THE BREADCRUMBS

Ralph jumped into my Inspired & Unstoppable Life Tribe, my group coaching program, with all fours, eager to figure out his life. He wrote to me, asking, "How do I find my calling?" Then he sprayed about a thousand questions without taking a breath.

"I'm overwhelmed," he wrote. "Should I do what makes sense to do? Should I do something I love? I don't know how to even do what I love. I don't know how to make any of this happen. And what do I tell my family? How do I make good money from doing whatever I choose? Where do I start with all of this?" Trust me, I am giving you the highlights here.

Breathe. Your internal guidance system will answer everything, but not all at once. Your mind craves information to reassure it. But transformation is the achievement you seek. You long to feel a knowing that cannot be taken away.

Your inner genius guides you a moment at a time. You receive a prompt or an awareness. Each nudge is a breadcrumb to follow to your gingerbread house. Each breadcrumb offers you a launching pad. One launching pad leads you to another.

Steve Jobs once said: "You can't connect the dots looking forward; you can only connect them looking backward. So you have to trust that the dots will somehow connect in your future." That means you have to collect some damn dots. You will not figure out every configuration of your life *before* you take a step.

The inspired path is *experiential.* You will be answered as you walk it, not as you talk about it. Some questions just can't be answered until you possess different psychological scaffolding within.

It's like taking a yoga class and wanting to immediately do one of the flashy peak poses for the cover of *Yoga Journal,* never mind that you've been glued to your couch for a decade. You are a bit, how shall we say, *plushy.* You don't yet possess the muscular infrastructure to accomplish the things you want to do. But you do possess the potential. You have many hidden muscles you have yet to fire up.

It's the same thing here. You are learning new ways to think and to see your world. The mind can think of an idea, but the soul is preparing you to embody it.

Back to Ralph. With every question he had came ten more questions. He was an octopus swimming and flailing, each leg grasping at water currents or passing fish. We've all been here. Grabbing at ideas, trying to find "the one answer" or perfect plan.

When you feel like a scrambling octopus, it's because you are using your lizard brain to answer questions of your wizard spirit. Our linear minds can't navigate the depths of love and mystery. **You may be analyzing and thinking, but you need to enter the domain of *feeling.*** Feelings can answer your questions. Thoughts will churn out more questions.

When I say feelings, I don't mean fleeting emotions. I mean your gut intuition, a quiet response that remains consistent. This means slowing down. Being honest. Staying only in the present moment. Maybe asking, *What do I really desire in this moment?* Or, *What feels right for me right now?* Nothing could be easier—or harder.

Let go of the ideas you have about what is safe, productive, or viable. You have no idea how much your assumptions (which you call good judgment) block your creativity and crème de la crème instincts. Follow *the heat*—the desire that gives you energy.

HONOR YOUR DESIRES

When you stop desiring, you start dying. In a study of rats, when scientists blocked the chemical connection to desire, the rats stopped eating, wanting sex, or ordering specialty cheese on the Home Shopping Network channel. And they died. Desire is the instinct of being alive. Desire is healthy.

You may be ignoring your desires instead of honoring them. You may feel like you need to protect yourself from suggestions that feel too easy or good, or make you giggle. You think they are frivolous, risky, or embarrassing. However, your life-force doesn't care what you think you "should" be. It only suggests what would give you life.

My client Willa said, "I keep having this one desire, but I don't want to listen to it. I am uncomfortable with it. I am drawn to it. It scares me out of my mind." Now that's a desire I want to hear about. That sucker has the power to kick down walls and move heaven and earth. That desire is a shift of identity.

Finding your calling is a path of *uncovering* your truth. It's not a path of *judging* it. "I just can't find my desire," said Sarah, a tired, overworked nurse. "I don't even want to paint or start a business or create my dream house or anything." But that wasn't true. Sarah did want something.

Sarah wanted time off. She wanted to stop the madness. That was her desire, but she didn't think that counted because it wasn't a career move. Yet it was her *next right* move. It was her breadcrumb.

Sarah arranged a modest trip. She wasn't tired at all when she started packing.

Just in case you struggle with following your desires, I offer you this reframe, a creed I wrote for myself.

THE CREED OF DESIRE

My desires are holy. I know this because they give me energy.

They are sources of strength, animation, secret rickshaws to other dimensions, and a will that always returns. Nothing else has this pull.

That's how I know there is something here that is alive.

I am following the code within. I am the servant of my nature. I am fulfilling a promise, leaning into a trajectory, taking instruction from the flashes of my soul. No one else knows this secret way. But the call knows the way.

I feel like this is learning how to pray.

This isn't some detour or delusion. This is the purpose of being alive. Choosing to follow love instead of fear, again and again.

I will serve my heart. I will serve this heat. I will serve a higher light than my opinionated, fact-gobbling, cognitive mind. I will be a monk who studies the scriptures of freedom in my veins, the pulse that pulls me.

I am here to say yes to myself. And no to what drains me.

I am here to say yes to whatever feeds my energy, because this is my task, my assignment, my responsibility. This is the divine I serve.

THE FORM OF YOUR LIFE IS NOT YOUR LIFE

In the middle of your storm, don't worry about the form or how your life looks. You are not aiming to be "normal," because, well, that might not even be on the menu, when you're conscious and original. Aim to feel alive.

We are trying out our chemistry sets. Taking on this grand experiment called life. We are daring to discover this intuitive relationship with our inner master of brilliance. We are beginning to trust the quantum field of what we love.

This journey may certainly look strange to others, and even to yourself. Yet it may be the first thing you have ever done in your life that doesn't exile you from your heart.

I get it. It's hard to give ourselves permission to play or experiment. Others might think we're floundering. We might *feel* like we're floundering, but only when we crave definition more than we crave self-discovery.

Maybe you are scoping out Zillow at odd hours, dreaming of moving *somewhere*. Or you're googling yoga teacher training courses, degree programs in biodiversity, or Zen meditation retreats in Sedona. You are dabbling in options, trying on how you want to spend your time on earth. Dreaming is fun. It's also uncomfortable as hell.

This is alchemy, transforming our everyday lives into intentional gold. Yet to the human eye it may look like we're just living in a studio apartment, becoming workshop junkies, or failing to save money for our impending doom.

"Do you have a plan?" people ask you. "What are you doing with your life?" You can't exactly say, "I'm healing generational trauma. I'm on the hero's journey. I'm rewiring my neurochemistry and cultivating a positivity bias. I'm finding my way back to the garden. Oh, and taking naps."

You'd go on as your interrogator began to twitch with tics. Or while they had clearly stopped listening, yet still held you hostage. "I'm opening up to the love of the Universe. I'm finding my calling and mission to be an inspiration to humanity. I am working with the parts of myself that need more love. I'm hunting the inviolate. I'm journaling."

You just can't say that to your brother-in-law, the judgy financial planner with the five-bedroom house. So you stuff yourself with his expensive quiche at dinner, then slide into *There is something wrong with me.*

Please know this. Many of us across the world applaud you for choosing truth over fear. We're on the same journey. Personally, I'm giving you an air high five. You've got the cojones to experiment with what will make you unshakable.

When we're in process, here's what we're doing. We are giving ourselves this holy time to reclaim the calling within, the desires that change how we see reality.

Trust yourself. Value your bold integrity. Some people will get it. Others won't. Soon, you won't even bother trying to explain yourself because you will *be* yourself. You will know a joy that glows, a jackpot of nirvana. Finally, it won't even matter what you're doing, because whatever it is, it's obviously working.

SELF-TRUST INQUIRY

What breadcrumb might be calling to you right now?
(Remember this doesn't even have to be related to whatever
goal you might be working on.)
When have you followed a breadcrumb in the past?

SELF-TRUST-ISMS

Follow Your Breadcrumbs

....

This is not a trip for tourists. This is the trip of travelers . . . There is a footpath to freedom that only you can find.

....

This is the price of freedom. You think for yourself. You feel your guidance. You trust your trip.

....

Happiness is dynamic. You are forever growing into who you are meant to be.

....

The inspired path is *experiential*. You will be answered as you walk it, not as you talk it.

....

My desires are holy. I know this because they give me energy. They are . . . secret rickshaws to other dimensions.

....

Your life-force doesn't care what you think you "should" be. It only suggests what would give you life.

10

The Life-Changing Power
of Rogue Choices

THE PRACTICE: Taking risks will grow and heal you. You may be playing it safe, which puts you in the unsafe position of numbness and disconnection. Dare the wild. **Your practice is to take a risk.** Remember, you are not looking for an answer for your lifetime. You are looking for the most enlivening choice in this moment. You are looking to feel the love and electricity of meeting your Self.

*It is only by risking our persons from
one hour to another that we live at all.*
—WILLIAM JAMES

*One event can awaken in us a stranger
completely unknown to us.
To live is to be slowly born.*
—ANTOINE DE SAINT-EXUPÉRY

Sometimes you can find a way when there is no way. It may not be a forever answer. It may not be the exact right train. It can be a lifeboat. Sometimes it's just a tiny orange life jacket in the middle of a roiling sea. It's not sustainable. Yet it sustains you. Your life jacket can be a circumstance or moment that promises some life. Like the first moment of dew in the desert that coaxes plants to believe there may yet be nurture.

I remember trying to cope with a broken heart. I felt like I was filled with broken glass. No, sour figs. I felt like I was dying. I couldn't even get myself to eat. Chicken lo mein, a favorite food, my favorite *taboo* food, sat on a shelf in my fridge, congealing in its unopened pristine little white carton.

It was the heavy gray blanket of grief, and I could barely move, much less be moved. Kir, my best friend and life partner of seven years, had broken my heart. He had left me to sleep with another woman, and my sense of a future and life blood went with him. I felt like someone had scraped my insides out. Yet I was supposed to get on with life, move into some reinvention now.

Pain will force you to let go of ordinary strategies. Pain will kick down your doors and bust up your resistance. Pain will help you to take risks, because at some point you have nothing to lose except the pain. Pain has saved my life more than once. This was one of those times.

So to continue the story, I found myself driving with Dimitri, a guy I met in a grocery store and barely knew, to Santa Fe, New Mexico. He was lean and handsome, but not the kind of guy that cared about your day. But he was a broker of the free. There are certain people you meet at the boundaries, on the edges, in the margins of your life. I think of them as ferrymen. They're not there to help you make a life. They are there to wake you up, teach you something, or throw you onto dry land where you can crawl to the next leg of your journey.

It seemed crazy to just go drive off in the middle of the night with this man, to go from Denver, Colorado, to Santa Fe, New Mexico, but I didn't care. I was broken. My vulnerability made me available to life. I am usually neurotically attached to my safety, but I was beginning to need a different kind of safety, a security that helped me feel as though life made sense.

I don't even remember anything about Dimitri or what we talked about during the car ride down. All I remember is this. We pulled off onto the side of the road at one point. Dimmed the headlights of the car. "Look up," he said. The sky was massive. Darker than I'd ever seen, and crammed with stars.

I felt as though someone had poured ice-cold water on my head, only it felt wondrous. It was as though life was suddenly wailing and vibrating in tune. I looked at that beauty in the middle of the night, standing at the side of an empty road, sagebrush tickling my ankles. Somehow, I knew I was going to make it. I knew I was going to get through this sad, bad time in my life.

I could still be *moved* by beauty. I may have been dying inside, emotions rotting away, but there was this presence, this wild, fierce shout of *yes* in life. While it still hurt my heart that I wasn't sharing this enchantment with my great love, or even a good friend, or someone I felt like I could really be me with, I took it in. I saw it. I knew that life was here and beckoning me.

I thought: *Here I am on an adventure. Here I am and I am saving my own life.* I felt proud of myself. I wasn't just a Jewish girl from Brooklyn who would only date investment bankers and surgeons and "risk" a peach accent wall in her dining room for excitement. I fell in love with my spirit.

I was the kind of woman who would try again. I was the kind of woman who would dare. I was the kind of woman who could meet a man in the produce section of a grocery store, looking at organic zucchini, and drive across a desert with him at night just a few weeks later. I was the woman who would go on even in confusion, terror, and heartbreak. I was a woman who could be bewildered—and yet who could still be moved.

I felt like I had ingested jimsonweed, some strange hallucinogen. It was the darkness of the sky. It was the gleam of the tiny stars, seeds, billions of them it seemed, like diamonds and fish in a strange ocean. There was something wild about it all, wild as a coyote or a lynx. Jaunty and free.

It really wasn't about the guy anymore. It wasn't even about New Mexico, which is the land of enchantment. I just know I had this jolt of hope, like a streak of a falling star. *You are going to get through this. You are all right. Your soul is extraordinary.* And this most of all: *Life is filled with unknown grace.*

There are moments in life when your soul announces itself. You discover these moments of love and alignment in ways you might not expect. I would have thought I wanted my ex to come home, bedraggled and contrite, seeing the error of his ways. Or that suddenly I'd meet a new man, a better man who'd whisk me into a better, cheeky life.

There are times in life when the most rational thing you can do is take a risk.

It was nothing like that. This was a ragged, mystical encounter. It was a tear in the fabric, where the veil wore thin. I stood there, off the side of a road in darkness, feeling exhausted in one moment, then redeemed by a billion stars. I sensed a passionate, raw God. An infinite, pure presence. I felt wickedly alive.

I don't think I would have ever experienced this if I hadn't started taking strikes and stabs at life. Pain had forced me. Pain had dulled me. Pain had cracked me open into spontaneity. I was venturing out. Trying anything that promised *anything*.

I just know that even the hope of having an adventure with Dimitri had made things better. I was sampling life beyond the borders I knew, the coordinates that had defined me. Part of me was limping. Part of me was galloping wild. I was starving for something I couldn't name. Starving for a reckoning not of this world, a feeling that could help me navigate this world. I burned with pain. I was burning bright.

That night I took the first new breath I'd taken in months. I felt this summons of beauty, an astonishing companionship. This grace was larger than my circumstances or my identity. I took in the night sounds of desert creatures. The huge, eerie stillness. I didn't even know this sky was here, right off the side of the road. It had existed all along.

At every moment I'd been living in Capitol Hill in Denver, or in New York City, this sky had been here, like a pond of wild magic. Through the hurly-burly of war, sickness, politics, breakups, and traffic, this presence had remained silent and available, waiting for the right time.

Maybe this is the love that some feel kneeling in church, or on a worn, thin prayer rug, or before a guru with blazing eyes. That magnificent sky enriched me. This presence that could quiet my heart and realign my cells. This presence threw me a life jacket and a belief in the goodness of life when I had none of my own.

Out there under that night sky, new thoughts rushed in, filling me with knowing. *I am going to be all right. I am going to choose life. I will always choose life. I will be broken and sad and I will choose life. I will not deny myself the chance to live.* I didn't fall in love with Dimitri, but I did fall in love with my spirit. I fell in love with me.

Years later, I am still grateful for this part of myself who was brave, reckless, and fiercely logical.

There are times in life when the most rational thing you can do is take a risk, a risk to save your own life, your inner life. Maybe my inner wisdom knew I needed to heal, and that healing will always ask us to become larger than we were before the damage. I needed to taste strange new berries. I needed to discover the wild life-force that was with me, even when it felt like every circumstance was changing, and even my own identity seemed unknowable.

I know I didn't even believe I knew how to heal at that time. But a part of me started following her animal instincts, feeling her way back to life like someone in the dark, feeling the walls of a cave. She was willing to risk mistakes. She was willing to just keep trying. And even when she still didn't know what she would do, she felt as though she had discovered herself and her spirit, and she knew it would be enough to get her through.

SELF-TRUST INQUIRY

What is a risk you feel called to take right now?
When have you done something bold in the past?
How did it expand you?

SELF-TRUST-ISMS

The Life-Changing Power of Rogue Choices

Pain will help you to take risks, because at some point you have nothing to lose except the pain.

I am usually neurotically attached to my safety, but I was beginning to need a different kind of safety, a security that helped me feel as though life made sense.

....

There are moments in life when your soul announces itself. You discover these moments . . . in ways you might not expect.

....

I was sampling life beyond . . . the coordinates that had defined me. Part of me was limping. Part of me was galloping wild.

....

I was starving for something I couldn't name. Starving for . . . a feeling that could help me navigate this world.

....

There are times in life when the most rational thing you can do is take a risk, a risk to save your own life, your inner life.

11

It's Your Movie, Adventure, and Pilgrimage

THE PRACTICE: If you really want to listen to yourself, throw out your past and future. Be reborn. Forget your ideas about what is safe. The truth is safe. Where are you being led, dragged, or tempted now? **Your practice is to give yourself permission to play.** Explore your new excitement or interest. Follow your energy instead of your identity, or who you think you should be. Self-discovery is a powerful adventure. Open to life's direction.

Play is the highest form of research.
—ALBERT EINSTEIN

Life is either a daring adventure or nothing at all.
—HELEN KELLER

Will you listen to who you are becoming now? I will tell you that this is a devotion—and the game of life. You are more than your current idea of yourself or existing circumstances. **Life calls us to**

expand. Life calls us to play. Often self-awareness and direction comes from having fun.

Some years ago, I gave myself permission to step into a new aspect of my identity. Changing how we see ourselves is usually the province of pilgrimages, retreats, years of intensive therapy, or ayahuasca and strange gurus in ponchos. I had my own quasi-awakening in an airport boutique.

I'd seen some winking blue stone necklace in the window, and it brought me into a den of possibilities. While flights took off and landed, I explored a secret fashion Shangri-La.

Before I knew it, I was trying on turtlenecks, necklaces, and furry sweaters. I was on a roll because when you get inspired, you start seeing possibilities everywhere—because that is the nature of inspiration.

Then there was this jacket. I didn't even see it. The salesclerk, my new blond drug dealer, brought it over. "It's your size," she said and casually put it in my hands—like delivering a child, a holy object, or a message. At first, I didn't immediately think, *Oh yes, this is for me.* But when I tried it on, I felt this inner electric jolt, as though I had a shot of heroin or Belgian chocolate mainlined into my brain. Okay, so *maybe* the jacket made me look thin. But it was more than that. The jacket made me look like somebody. *Like somebody else.*

I was bewitched by the woman invoked by this garment. She was confident. She owned the room. She was *definitely* from Manhattan, in the old days when Manhattan was power, fashion, and in your face, better than everyone everywhere without apology. I loved this icon of strength I found in myself. She also made me nervous.

Truth is, for years, I shrank when I was around people who owned their power. I envied their assurance. It's possible I may have judged them a teensy-weensy bit. So I wondered if this jacket might make others feel uncomfortable around me.

"Who does she think she is?" I imagined these clucking women pointing at me, at a speaking event where I might wear this jacket. "She looks a little full of herself, doesn't she? She's, like, not that famous or anything. Well, if she's doing so well, then how come she's speaking here?"

The jacket's ticket price was also big, bossy, and maybe stark-raving mad. I started feeling as though I should get "realistic." I didn't want to spend money, look haughty, and draw negative attention to myself. Besides, I speak at wellness and spiritual events as well as at business ones. I enjoy being seen as open and approachable. Maybe I'd be better off in something run-of-the-mill. Or a loincloth, manufactured in a socially responsible way.

But the heroin buzz of seeing the jacket on me brought me to my senses, *my new senses*. I wanted to feel that good. I wanted to trust feeling good. Then I started to wonder: *Why do I need the approval of strangers? Why would I assume negative reactions? Isn't it possible that if I felt good, I would show up with even more love, presence, and mastery? And isn't it a tiny bit deranged to let people who don't exist—at an event that doesn't exist—matter more to me than my own desires?*

I felt this rush of permission overtake me. This jacket offered me the chance to embody another dimension of myself. I felt powerful in it. I felt possibility. I felt love. Clearly the jacket was some kind of spiritual guide. I was having a shamanic soul retrieval in a dressing room mirror. This was fabulous. I didn't even have to hike into a desert. *Now I can totally justify the price tag of this jacket.*

I know I'm not alone in worrying about how other people will react to choices that I make. We all have a hard-wired evolutionary protection mechanism that directs us to fit in. You don't want to stand apart from the herd and risk attack. Beware the woolly mammoth *who, by the way, can I just say*, loves the satin on that jacket.

I also know that the jacket made me question my identity. Secretly, I always felt as though I walked through life like a kite that got torn in the wind. I ached to soar, but I felt underequipped. I didn't feel comfortable dressing as though I had my chimichangas together.

What if all my seeming identity is just a story I tell myself?

Because of my insecurity, I've always been sensitive to others who might feel the same way. I've never wanted anyone to feel less about themselves in my presence. I want everyone to know that hey, you can wear spaghetti sauce on your sweater when you're with me. You can drop your plate. You don't have to be able to cross your t's and dot your i's. Baby, you can drool. You are safe with me.

But what if I'm not just a support ostrich? What if I've been shaming my peacock? Because truth be known, I also like to strut and make questionably loud sounds. I'm a lead singer in my mind. What if I'm sort of both an ostrich and a peacock? What if I'm neither? What if I'm just stardust cycling through? What if I am no one form or category or box to check on a questionnaire?

The Buddhists say that I am not my idea of my identity. I am "no self." **What if all my seeming identity is just a story I tell myself? What if I could step in and out of stories as I please?** What if I am the beautiful light that is beneath all the stories? What if we all are? I think we all are.

A friend of mine reminds me that Spirit is a bit of a showoff when it comes to expression. "How can you doubt that God's a multimedia artist?" she says. "Have you ever looked at the inside of a calla lily? Or why are there, like, four billion species of flowers or zebras and horses and rainbow fish?" Maybe God, that mystery essence, doesn't have just one statement, outlet, or outfit. Maybe love is a limitless expression unless we limit it.

That day in the airport, I gave myself permission to buy the jacket because it made me feel plugged in to something alive. It was just a piece of cloth, but it made me feel like I had found my animal skins, my power animal, my vibration, my fashion body, much like the healers who talk about the energy that surrounds the physical. I gave myself permission to be unpredictable. To have adventures, to be *that* woman. I committed to listening to my delight more than to my conditioning.

PLAY, PLAY, PLAY . . .

For me, self-discovery often comes through play. I think we have to try on different parts of ourselves in order to behold new capacities. I remember when I first began my career transition, I followed a wild nudge to get a part-time job waiting tables. I wanted to serve nachos and curly fries and talk to people.

I didn't care that I had graduated cum laude from Harvard Law School and there were certain "expectations" that went with that. I wanted to be free. I had left my job in the fancy downtown law firm to explore writing. I wanted a part-time job that helped me experience something new in life, and something that didn't feel as heavy.

At the Paradise Café, I wore long feather earrings and a black apron with the company's logo. *You can't be a waitress,* the responsible one within me barked. The imagemonger within me began to freak out and sweat at the thought. I felt fear when I imagined what other lawyers and 99.9 percent of my family might think. Still, a budding freedom junkie within me directed, *This is your movie. Go for it.*

My adventure in waiting tables was awesome, and I learned to say awesome. I came to realize I loved people and could make them laugh. That gave me the confidence to become a public speaker years later.

More important, waiting tables helped me own my power—not lose it.

I didn't let my past dictate what I could have in my present. I remembered that I'd gone to law school to give myself *more* opportunities in life, not *fewer* opportunities. That meant every choice was on the table for me. I allowed myself to choose freedom and fun.

I am still learning to give myself permission to "follow my energy" and make choices that unsettle the current regime of my identity. This is my dusty globe trot, my time on earth, and I want to be available to all the Baskin-Robbins flavors that beckon me.

Saying yes to that which calls me is a spiritual devotion. It's not hedonism or the zigzags of someone who can't make up her mind. It's the willingness to be humble enough to accept my strength—in all its forms. I am following a spirit that is always teaching me new things about myself—and about all of us.

Years after I bought the jacket in the airport store, I found this quote from Beyoncé, the megawatt pop singer. "Your self-worth is determined by you. You don't have to depend on someone telling you who you are." I grinned inside. I know Beyoncé would have bought the jacket.

SELF-TRUST INQUIRY

What part of you is being called to play and play out loud?
When have you done this?
What did you learn?

SELF-TRUST-ISMS

It's Your Movie, Adventure, and Pilgrimage

If you really want to listen to yourself, throw out your past and future. Be reborn.

Forget your ideas about what is safe. The truth is safe.

What if all my seeming identity is just a story I tell myself? What if I could step in and out of stories as I please?

Life calls us to expand. Life calls us to play.

I remembered that I'd gone to law school to give myself *more* opportunities in life, not *fewer* opportunities.

This is my dusty globe trot, my time on earth, and I want to be available to all the Baskin-Robbins flavors that beckon me.

12

To Thine Own Self Be True— and Be Blown Away

THE PRACTICE: Trusting yourself is an inner pilgrimage— not a conventional path of ordinary actions. You are in conversation and cocreation with a larger wisdom. If you follow this inner voice, you will have results you could not have achieved any other way. But do not insist on external or familiar criteria of certainty. Your wisdom offers its own language of certainty. **Your practice is to pay close attention to the times you recognize the communication of your spirit.** This love calms your doubts.

Miracles happen when you learn to trust your intuition, a gift from the Higher Self.
—SUSAN JEFFERS

The Holy Spirit is invisible, but you can see the results of His Presence, and through them, you will learn that He is there.
—*A Course in Miracles*

The life of listening to your inspired Source goes a little something like this. You are in a relationship with a maddening love. But this love is not visible to the human eye. And yet, you will see the effects. You will know the truth. There is a signature of the extraordinary. Plus, you will experience and achieve things you could never, ever do on your own. So there's that.

Sometimes I lose touch with what I know inside. I find myself wondering, *Am I really connected to the Universe? Am I safe? Is this real?* Then, *huzzah,* the Oneness returns, speaking its love language, and perspective slams into me—and I see how the events in my life tingle with order and precise meaning. I am infused with certainty. I will never doubt the power again. Sort of.

Still, I'm a skeptic with a bad sweet tooth for proof. I "forget" my quasi-miracles. I question the constancy of this secret collaborator. It could be that I am spiritually anemic, requiring daily transfusions. I always want more. I want reality to behave in a way I can control. Or in a way that science confirms, so that I don't have to think for myself. Still, I'm feverishly drawn to this path of fluctuating magic. I have a feeling that it's not this magic that fluctuates. It's my conviction and receptivity.

I do know this. This love presence does not conform, but it also doesn't contract. I am being shown again and again a reality I can rely on.

Just when I'm about to give up on believing in my instincts and this path, when I'm at the end of my inner rope, something moves. I am answered—and I know I am in a sweet conversation with my life. I am touched. My world clicks into place. I feel phenomenally free.

Sometimes, I realize I am clinging to a *lack of belief* with such faith it is astonishing.

WILL YOU KEEP YOUR PROMISE TO YOURSELF?

When I was a teenager, I knew what I wanted. I didn't know the specifics or the how, but in high school, I realized I might want to write. I'd read *The Catcher in the Rye* and a portal opened for me. *I want this,* I said inside. I didn't even know what "this" was. I did know that creative writing was the only subject that felt like Mardi Gras to me. I romped into that classroom straight after social studies, and purple beads fell from the ceiling, and I wanted to rip open my shirt and pray that this party would never end.

However, after majoring in English in college, I decided to be "practical," like my orthodox Jewish parents insisted. I planned to become an attorney and then explore writing on the side, or later. It was a good plan. My college career counselor loved it! He beamed at me as I casually put my true calling on the back burner. I am convinced now that people like this should be put on the back burner. But, whatever.

In law school, I felt like I was drowning. I watched my classmates argue about legislative policies, plaintiffs' rights, or antitrust violations in their free time. Who were these people? They *wanted* to be lawyers. I told myself, *Remember the plan. Get the money. Then you can write.*

But some part of me was afraid I'd forget. I was afraid I'd drink the Kool-Aid—or the martinis. Maybe I'd be punch-drunk on the salary or crushed and numbed by the workload. Then I wouldn't care about writing about dragonflies. I wouldn't see dragonflies. I wouldn't notice life. I would lose the keycode to the creative realm.

One warm spring day, I leaned against the trunk of a massive oak in Harvard Yard. Someone tossed a red frisbee to their friend. Up against that tree, I wrote myself a note. I wanted to remember for all time my desire and my intention. I scrawled: *Don't forget me. Remember, to Thine Own Self Be True. Don't forget this promise to yourself to write.* I tucked the note into my journal.

Now, if this were a movie, the scene would go black or cut to me at a cherry wood desk in a law firm, files and law books piled high, me with pale skin and tired eyes. There would be a dead plant on my desk.

THE UNIVERSE ANSWERS IN ITS OWN SWEET TIME

Flash forward. I'm lying in my bed and it's after 11 A.M. I've left my position as a litigator at Sherman & Howard, the law firm where I had worked. I didn't stay long enough to "make the money" as I had originally planned.

My fears are raging. I'm thinking I am a nutjob who has trashed her reputation and career trajectory by believing in hunches and pixie dust. I've read a damn mountain of self-help books that tell me, "You create your own reality." Or "Follow your bliss," and the money comes. But on this day of fault-finding and self-cruelty, I am questioning the bliss of my bliss.

I'm forgetting all the talk about staying present and following my breadcrumbs. I am forgetting that I'm "in process," like healers and therapists say as they hand you incredibly tangible bills. That day, I consider that maybe I'm not "called." Maybe I'm just spectacularly naive. My inner critic is having a field day, ranting: *You don't need faith. You need sanity. Instinctive mysterious powers are for people who live in Peru. It's time to stop dreaming and get real.*

When we dare to leave behind conventional wisdom in favor of inner wisdom, most will wobble. We believe, and then we question. If you're like me, when you're changing your life, you question hard. This was one of those days. My fears churned like a tornado. One doubt led to another and another, and soon the force could have swept up a firetruck or a mall.

What if I wasn't a good-enough writer? What if I couldn't find a way to make a living? I thought about my colleagues from law school, making gazillions, and some making history as well. No one was writing poems about peaches. What if my thirst for *something more* was ludicrous? What if I was wasting my time?

Sometimes, I realize I am clinging to a <u>lack of belief</u> with such faith it is astonishing.

I don't remember how later that day I found what I now call "the Love Note from my Soul." I must have been reading through old journals, hunting for writing topics. But there it was, written years ago, a plea, a note in a bottle cast into the ocean of years. It was the note I'd written to myself while at law school. *Don't forget about me. To Thine Own Self Be True.* In my own handwriting.

I burst into tears. *I was being true to myself.* I was doing it! I was on my path. I was on my own kind of pilgrimage, so to speak, like those who walk the famous Camino, sweating, grunting, and aching. Yes, it was a tiny bit gut-wrenching, but I was waking up. I wasn't dismissing my desires and truth and just living on autopilot like I had been before. I'd committed to seeing where my inner truth could lead me, so I'd know once and for all.

Time wrapped around itself in full circle. I remembered that young woman who had leaned against the tree and begged me not to forget her need to write. I was an answer to her prayer. *She was an answer to my prayer.* The cavalry had arrived. I clutched that note and I squealed out loud as though I had won the lottery. No, I didn't win a boatload of cash, but it *was* a boatload of validation and internal security.

All I can say is that note was confirmation—of my instincts to write, and my willingness to ride out this roller coaster of trust. The Buddhists call this verifying faith, the next stage from bright faith. I just couldn't dismiss the *timing* of finding that note. It was like praying, *if you're real show me a sign or a falling star,* and then opening your eyes to a cascade of light—in the middle of the day, in front of your window. Sure, you could say it's a coincidence, but if it was, it was one *hell* of a coincidence.

I felt seen. I wasn't alone. The Great Friend had just thrown me a rope, a bone, a lightning bolt. This energy was tracking me. *Something amazing was happening here.* Everything felt larger than anything I knew how to make happen through ordinary efforts. I was sold. At least for that moment, I was done selling myself short.

To write it now, the whole experience sounds hokey, but it's like the old line you say about a great joke: you just had to be there. It was *holy*—a wild, fresh jolt of perfection. It wasn't exactly a loaves-and-fishes situation. Definitely on the spectrum though. Finding that note seemed *intentional.* I experienced this surge of love, certainty, and peace. For me, that trifecta is the Presence.

You have a singular journey to walk in this lifetime. **You have promises to yourself that only you can keep.** Your desires are doorways into another realm of living. Love will usher you every step of the way when you pay attention to your guidance instead of your resistance.

I am so grateful I kept my promise to my soul. I kept this promise to you who is reading this. Maybe I kept this promise to help you keep your promises. I still don't know how this funky light magic works. I just know that it does.

SELF-TRUST INQUIRY

What is a promise to yourself you feel called to keep right now?
When and how have you felt "funky light magic"
or a communication from your spirit?

SELF-TRUST-ISMS

To Thine Own Self Be True—and Be Blown Away

I have a feeling that it's not this magic that fluctuates. It's my conviction and receptivity.

This love presence does not conform, but it also doesn't contract. I am being shown again and again a reality I can rely on.

Sometimes, I realize I am clinging to a *lack of belief* with such faith it is astonishing.

Everything felt larger than anything I know how to make happen through ordinary efforts. I was sold.

You have promises to yourself that only you can keep. Your desires are doorways into another realm of living.

Love will usher you every step of the way when you pay attention to your guidance instead of your resistance.

13

You Can't Get This Wrong

THE PRACTICE: Maybe you secretly believe you are in the wrong life or you always make wrong choices. You paralyze yourself with indecision. Self-criticism is toxic. It poisons your instincts. Your intuition grows with use. What if you really do know exactly what to do in each moment? What if you're right? **Your practice is to trust your vision—more than your suspicion.** This choice will take you further than you could ever imagine.

*You can wait, delay, or paralyze yourself,
or reduce your creativity to almost nothing.
But you cannot abolish it.*
—*A Course in Miracles*

*I wouldn't change a thing about what I've done
in the past because what may have been bad
choices have all led me to this moment.*
—MINNIE DRIVER

I have been haunted for as long as I can remember. *You're doing it wrong. You're doing it wrong. You are in the wrong life. You are wrong. Wrong. Wrong. Wrong. What if you're wrong? What if you're wasting time?* It's a bad song that played in the back of my brain and I couldn't tune it out. It was heavy metal combined with a polka and believe me, it didn't work as a song, and it sure as hell didn't help me sing my song.

Finally, I got to thinking that this questioning part of me was not protecting me but was disabling my ability to see what was possible. These weren't good questions. This wasn't a beneficial guide.

It's like listening to a Russian grandmother who tells you to wear your sweater when it's a hundred degrees outside with a humidity level of 400 percent. She means well, but she is seeing Siberian tundra when you're skipping to the beach. She is not a fan of bliss: *bubula,* your happiness is the indicator of danger and bad judgment.

What if you're doing it wrong? What if you make a mistake? This inner worrier kept me removed from the joy of being. Doubt robbed me of oxygen. It kept me hanging back, which made me feel like I was falling behind, which made me think I had even more reason to doubt myself and never try new things. It's amazing what we do to ourselves, isn't it?

Of course, I also had these bad fantasies that everyone else knew exactly what to do. Other people held picnics on red-checked tablecloths with Austrian crystal goblets, celebrating their good decisions and excellent lives. They were born knowing what to do. They decided things in seconds. Even when something didn't work out, they didn't turn on themselves with a crowbar or an icepick or start muttering in tongues. There would be no rocking back and forth in the closet.

No, these fantasy people *hired* someone to help. They had teams of support. "Why not?" they said to themselves the minute a desire arose, as they bounded forward into implementation, enjoying every detail of their own creation. These people leaned back in hot tubs in the glow of a silver moon, on a planet they found effortless to navigate. I hated these fantasy people, and I hated myself for not being one of them.

I have a feeling I know where all this *I am doing it wrong, I am wrong* business started for me. I grew up watching my mother's insecurity about herself. It's a psychic scarf she gave me and draped around my shoulders.

My mother *always* thought she was wrong and stupid. My father criticized her constantly. He made her feel incompetent. My mother did make misinformed, nervous, ill-thought-out choices. She would have been horrible on a witness stand, changing her mind, her position, her allegiance to herself.

But I have decided to end the lineage here. I am taking off that scarf. It is the part of me that *thinks* she's doing something wrong that makes me insecure enough to abandon myself. Because of insecurity, I have chosen things that are less worthy of me, not to mention relationships (please, let's not mention relationships).

Because of insecurity, I didn't believe in the choices I'd made and didn't give them the care and commitment they deserved. I didn't show up with undiluted focus. I'd interrogate myself, raking myself over the coals, and evaluating things *in the middle* of doing them instead of taking stock at the end.

I wasn't being magical, leaping into the stream of genius, and I wasn't being organized and strategic either. Nor was I combining them. Nope. I just kept changing my position. I was scuttling back and forth between the two and failing in both.

Author Yann Martel, who wrote *Life of Pi,* once said, "To choose doubt as a philosophy of life is akin to choosing immobility as a means of transportation." Maybe I can tattoo this onto my backbone.

Meanwhile, I'm done berating myself, being round-shouldered, and triple-guessing my every move—while seeking happiness and confidence, mind you. Those undercutting strategies might feel familiar, but they will never grow my strength. They will not take me to the heliport of full potential.

Trailblazers in the personal development arena say we are making up this life. At the very least we are making up the story we tell ourselves. Well, I am going to tell myself a better story. I choose the narrative that expands me.

I begin with this white-hot truth. **I am in my right life. I am guided. I am making the absolute best choices I can make for myself at this time.**

It's stunningly powerful to believe that you are making the right choices. I use this lens in my coaching practice. As someone shares their situation, I am there to witness, bless, and reveal the possible. I do not see anything wrong. That doesn't mean I deny pain or challenges or a call to rise into more skillful behaviors.

It means I listen with the absence of judgment. The cessation of attack. Together we gaze with the eyes of potential. I look at my clients' lives to see what's right, what's working, what's moving in the right direction. We leverage that force. We ride that current. We keep moving, refining, and discovering.

I can tell you, we set free the genie. Because there is always this animating genius that arises from the application of love, patience, and curiosity.

How can you invest in your possibilities when you keep feeding suspicion instead of vision? When I wrote my first book, which happened to take a mere twelve years, give or take a few lifetimes, I actually had people say to me, "Are you still talking about that?" As though it was unrealistic to keep trusting in myself for that long.

One author even said to me, "Maybe if it hasn't happened by now, it's not right for you." And just in case I wasn't doubting myself enough at the time, feeling mildly nauseous because maybe I was kidding myself instead of growing myself, he said, "I'm just giving you a reality check," then walked away self-assured as a yardstick. Let us pray he tripped on something or his huge ego later that night, because I believe in a loving Universe.

And God, I hope he reads this because I'd like to tell him about the reality checks I cashed because of that book. Not to mention every moment of joy that came with realizing my dreams.

I think we're supposed to face doubts. I think we're supposed to dream big things. I think we're meant to go into territory that makes us question our sanity. The best of us will keep going, even when it's hard. Because real change is worth it.

I think about the Civil Rights Movement, women's rights, everyone's rights, or the research to heal incurable diseases or stop world hunger. Progress takes time. And faith. And commitment. And action. And the lack of perpetual doubt. This isn't delusional. This is intentional.

The less you listen to doubt, the more intuitive you become.

A mentor of mine once said that empowerment comes from asking better questions. So I'm dropping my old song: What if I'm doing it wrong? I'm asking better questions: What if I'm choosing right? Who would I be if I believed I was always making the absolute best choices for myself at the time? Who would I be if I believed I couldn't get this wrong? What would I choose now?

Walking an inspired path, following steps that emerge from within, has forced me to become courageous. Inner arguments have kept me small. I find courage by trusting that I am cocreating with my life. *I can't get this wrong.* I can't because I am in partnership with deep sentient wisdom or divine loving intelligence.

I have an inner teacher, a connection to a fluid, ever-creative authority that knows a hell of a lot more than I ever learned at Harvard. I work with Jefe (Spanish for "boss") or Teacher, the names I sometimes call my radical inner life-shifter. I always have a knowing.

Love informs and teaches me. Even my painful circumstances teach me. When I listen to this compassionate intelligence within, every circumstance is helpful. Everything is moving me in the best direction. And it is love that keeps me moving.

I can't explain how I know something. Yet that's the nature of trust and faith. I give this authority my attention, because when it comes right down to it, I'm a light-chaser. I know I'd regret not listening to this inner power. I would always be haunted, always wondering: What if I had believed in myself a little more? This is a better question, by the way.

I am in the right life. I can't get this wrong. I am making the absolute best choice I can make at this time. These are holy words of self-allegiance and I allow myself to be anointed by their power. I'm placing this shawl upon my shoulders. Like Jews put on a tallis. Like priests put on vestments. Or like one of those anti-anxiety blankets people use to comfort quivering Chihuahuas when there's thunder or fireworks, or basically they're being Chihuahuas.

I will put on this shawl of love. I will drape it around my shoulders. It is weightless. It is weighty. It is a paradigm changer. It is what I am leaning into.

What will you believe about your decisions? Here's my suggestion. Start off from a position of power. **The less you listen to doubt, the more intuitive you become.** Even if you learn where you might do it differently next time, this is knowledge and expertise. New opportunities are on their way.

This is what I often tell clients: "Stop holding back your knowing, and you will stop holding back your showing." You won't get this wrong. You have continuous chances as long as you're alive. You are meant to unpack and develop your true wisdom and direction. This is the system of being you.

SELF-TRUST INQUIRY

How would it feel to know
you couldn't get this wrong?
Or that you are making exceptional choices?
What choice would you make right now?

SELF-TRUST-ISMS

You Can't Get This Wrong

It is the part of me that *thinks* she's doing something wrong that makes me insecure enough to abandon myself.

I'm done berating myself, being round-shouldered, and triple-guessing my every move—while seeking happiness and confidence, mind you.

I am in my right life. I am guided. I am making the absolute best choice I can make for myself at this time.

How can you invest in your possibilities when you keep feeding suspicion instead of vision?

The less you listen to doubt, the more intuitive you become.

I'm a light-chaser. I know I'd regret not listening to this inner power. I would always be haunted . . . What if I had believed in myself a little more?

KICKSTARTS AND PRACTICES

Have at it. Play with these. Trust yourself. Go where you're guided . . .

Pick Three Self-Trust-isms from Part III. Journal about them. Maybe make some art. Meditate or reflect on the words that spoke to you. Discuss them with someone else. Let these chosen phrases unlock a new awareness and conversation within.

1. **Burning Down the Hows.** Share with a friend or in your journal: If money weren't an issue, what would you love to do? Talk *only about what you desire*, not about why you can't have it. Feed the heat. Do not figure out how to make anything happen. This is an exercise in building energy.
2. **Create Your Movie.** Be the director. What ultimate story do you want the main character—you—to experience? See this time in your life as a scene. How does this scene help the character?
3. **Consider Your Inner Breadcrumb.** Maybe your "breadcrumb" is healing from an old story, negative

FROM SELF-DOUBT TO SELF-TRUST

beliefs, or grief. What is your soul asking you to shift so that you can move forward?

4. **The Guide of Loving Adventure Comes to You.** Picture this guide. This guide asks you three questions. (1) What sounds fun for you right now? (2) What have you always wanted to do? (3) What are you curious about?

5. **Break a Desire into Breadcrumbs.** Write your microactions toward a desire. Post this reminder: *I follow my breadcrumbs. Each one gives me new instruction.*

6. **Write Your Own Holy Writ of Power.** Own that you have been called. You are guided. You are listening. Imagine and write the instructions for your mission right now.

PART IV

From Perceived Failures to Self-Forgiveness

IT'S A BRAND-NEW DAY

THE BLOCK: Perceived Failures
THE BREAKTHROUGH: *Self-Forgiveness*

YOU GET IN YOUR OWN WAY
when you perceive your life as full of mistakes.

YOU DISCOVER YOUR OWN WAY
when you forgive yourself and others.

~

You may not trust yourself because you think you've made mistakes. You think you are permanently flawed or inferior. Superglued to debilitating outcomes. But honey, this nonsense is not your identity.

What if "mistakes" mark where you haven't hit your highest—because you haven't been loving toward yourself?

Self-trust comes from forgiving yourself—giving yourself another chance. Your best life strategy isn't to figure out what you did wrong, how you are wrong, and how your life is wrong. You are not here to call out all the unlovable parts of yourself. They are not unlovable. *They are unloved.* Unloved by you.

I invite you to step onto holy ground. Open to your new story.

In this section we look at how to begin again like never before—in true expression. Because you are a light. Nothing from the past blocks your future—unless you let it.

14

Anything Is Possible Now

THE PRACTICE: It's exhausting to not forgive yourself. You may be dragging around an image of when you didn't get it right. But your mistake is not your identity. You are the light in this present moment. You can still grow. If you carry self-judgment forward, you will not act from love and strength. **Your practice is to see yourself as the one who grew from the mistake, rather than the one who made a mistake.**

Through your forgiveness does the truth about yourself return to your memory. Do you not begin to understand what forgiveness will do? It will remove all sense of weakness, strain, and fatigue from your mind.
—A Course in Miracles

Can the world seem bright and clear and safe and welcoming, with all my past mistakes oppressing it, and showing me distorted forms of fear?
—A Course in Miracles

A Course in Miracles teaches that your true nature is never tired. Maybe you yawn as you read the sentence. It says: "You are not capable of being weary. But you are capable of wearying yourself through the strain of constant judgment." Feel familiar? Constant judgment. Maybe against yourself. That's why forgiveness awakens you more than a thermos of Starbucks or a bucket of Adderall.

I always thought that something in the future would save me. My bad opinions of myself, the broken carnival within, would change because of some new circumstance, situation, or person. But really, I will keep going through a revolving door until I break free of my own condemnation. That's because self-judgment doesn't end—*until we end it*. It's an inside maneuver.

Maybe it's not our future that saves us. Maybe it's our past, understood anew.

In every spiritual tradition, forgiveness plays a starring role. I guess you can't tap your own light while you're holding on to blight: constant ugly thoughts like Japanese beetles that destroy your garden.

I remember being a little girl, walking with the congregants of my synagogue down the block to cast stones into a nearby bay. It was the beginning of the Jewish New Year, Rosh Hashanah, and this was the Tashlikh ceremony—a ritual of atonement. It was understood that we were asking a higher power to forgive us for anything we did wrong. Maybe it was just me, or maybe I missed some scriptural memo, but as I kept focusing on all my "sins" and cast pebbles into the water, I always felt more guilty than relieved.

In recent years, I've rethought this ritual. These days I believe I am asked to forgive myself. I am asked to let go of the black stones I carry in my heart. I am asked to let go of shame, resentment, or anger against myself as well as grievances I nurture against others. I am worth far more than my pain would have me believe. But

I need to cast off these millstones if I want to become who I am meant to be.

It is the same for you. You are worthy of grace. You are called to drop the image or memory of your less resilient self. You are holding this idea of yourself more closely than the truth.

The truth of you is who you are now and the unending love within you. Truth is always a relief. It's always a song, a return, a remembrance. But how do you cast your stone aside? How do you free yourself from pain? Stop nurturing your judgment. Stop nurturing the blame.

There are times you did not hit your note. Did not act with awareness or integrity. But this is not who you are. It bothers you *because* it is not who you are. This false image undermines your truth.

Do what you can to make things right or closer to it. Ask yourself, what can I do now to repair this or learn from this? One of the ways to make this right is to stop bludgeoning yourself for what you did wrong.

Are you willing to see yourself as worthy of love? Are you willing to hold that light for others? I know some of you might not have jumped up out of your seats with a "hell yes." That's okay. Forgiveness is a lifelong process.

Today, if you're feeling devastated or enraged, this might not be your time. There is a right time. You will know it. Because when it's the right time for you, it will be exhausting to *not* do it.

FORGIVING YOURSELF ISN'T INDULGENCE. IT'S NOT A FREE PASS.

Forgiveness isn't a way of getting off the hook. It's a way of getting off the dime and moving forward in your life. It's not just giving yourself a pass. Forgiveness is an act of purification, a hygiene of the mind. It does no good to relive stories from the past. We are here to create a new story.

It is not over. The world begins right now, if you wish.

We are here *to be* a new story. We represent a stream of love. This is the possibility you possess while you're alive. *You can do things differently.* You can also understand yourself differently.

If I carry my guilt or resentment forward, I will not act from love. I will not rise in love. I will not listen to the stunning holy vibrato within me. I will kneel at the altar of self-harm more than at the altar of tulips, growth, and renewal. I will miss my greatest opportunity.

Our guilt or anger can cause us more harm than the original travesty. In the past we may have lapsed in awareness or ability, but now we study the mistake, the miss-take, and we cast concrete over our past actions. **We become the mistake, instead of the learning that comes from the mistake.**

Thich Nhat Hanh, the gentle Vietnamese Buddhist monk, told a story of an American vet who could not forgive himself because he had murdered innocent children in the course of war. He could not stop torturing himself with this memory. Thich Nhat Hanh reminded this sad man that right now there were children dying every minute because of lack of medicine or clean water. The monk reminded the soldier that he could help the children who were still alive and needed help now. He couldn't bring back the children who had died, but he could help other children.

The same is true for you. Your lack of self-forgiveness may keep you stuck. This lack prevents you from doing the good you can do now. Your contribution is more productive than your regret. The planet doesn't need your regret. It needs your enthusiasm, and your willingness to keep showing up for life.

What if you could forgive yourself for the sake of those who need you now?

I'm voting for your healing instead of your hurting.

WE CAN'T GROW IF WE DON'T FALL

I have always loved this quote attributed to the Baal Shem Tov: "Let me fall if I must fall. The one I become will catch me." I love being reminded that I am moving into wholeness, even when I drop the ball. This is so much better than how it feels to have some grammar teacher leave red marks all over your paper, like welts. The Universe is not a grammar teacher, but a teacher of love.

Falling down in life is part of growing. I don't love that system, though I do love the earned insights I have now. I've made many choices that I've looked back on, saying to myself, perhaps a tad uncourteously, *Were you on acid?* Still, I've evolved into someone I kind of like hanging out with.

Wabi sabi is a Japanese concept that is sometimes translated as "finding the perfection of imperfection." I am a *wabi sabi* master. Some of my greatest strength has come from the places where I chose an action I regret, or dated someone whom no one in their right mind should have dated. Let's just say that life is the kind of artist that can use junkyard dreck and turn out exquisite pieces—eventually.

This is a journey of becoming. It's not about being some crazy illusion of perfect. It's about adapting, scraping our way out of circumstances, healing, and becoming who we are meant to be. What if when we're struggling, we need more self-love, not less? Besides, what if we *must* fall? What if that's how we become self-aware? Really, what if it's how we grow our wings or become life coaches? *The one I become will catch me.*

What are you holding on to? Here's a few to get you thinking:

I'm too fat to be loved or successful. I took the money. I always bail when it comes to staying with something I care about. I said something horrible. I am responsible for their pain. I am bad. There is nothing that will ever change. What comes up for you?

Where do you make yourself tired with the same story? Over and over. You may not even hear it. Yet you can become self-aware enough to bring it to the light.

Will you consider letting go of this story? Forgiveness is the experience of opening our hearts again to innocence—for ourselves or someone else. It's an astonishing leap of consciousness. It's okay if you don't know how. Here's what I ask you: Are you *willing* to have a new experience? This is your turning point. Ask yourself this: *Am I willing to see things differently?*

I wrote this invocation for you, me, and maybe the other ungainly members of brilliant humanity. (Note: the "you" in this invocation refers to Spirit, or your higher wisdom, or whatever energy of transformation works for you. Also note: you may need to remind yourself of your willingness to shift your story often. This is not a linear process. It is a miraculous one though.)

I AM WILLING TO SEE THIS DIFFERENTLY

I give you my story. I place it on the altar of transformation. I surrender my insistence of what I think it means about me and my life. I take responsibility for the meaning I am giving this.

I surrender my insistence that I can't see this differently. This can't be made different. I am alone. I am screwed. I am coming to the party too late. I am coming apart at the seams.

I am willing to be surprised. I am willing to be restored to brightness. I am willing to undo my attack on myself or someone else. I am willing to undo my idea of what is possible. I am willing to be a clean slate. I am willing to experience the unimaginable power of new perspective.

I am willing to become available to miracles. I am willing to be like a child and bring you my broken toy and say, "Fix it." And I'm willing to have you fix it. I know that fixing it may mean I don't get the toy back. I get my life back. I get an understanding or shift or a standing in a new world, a new possibility. I may receive something sweeter, something I did not even know enough to ask for.

I am willing to love, even if I don't understand how. My usual sense of understanding is the filter of the small. The mystery is sweeping with a design beyond my comprehension. But not beyond my knowing.

I am willing to awaken and experience something new.

I am willing to see this situation differently.

I am willing to see myself differently.

What would it be like to let go of your mistakes or challenges and begin again? Please consider not identifying with your pain. Or calcifying around a lapse of love in your life. This is not your identity.

Please don't give a misinterpretation more importance than your essence. You are light and nothing less than light will ever stick to you. You can choose again. *You must choose again.* A spiritual life is a life of being in the present and expanding in expression and contribution.

It is not too late. It is not over.

The world begins right now, if you wish.

SELF-TRUST INQUIRY

What story about yourself (or someone else)
would you like to forgive?
Do you have a little willingness to see this differently?

〜

SELF-TRUST-ISMS

Anything Is Possible Now

....

You are called to drop the image or memory of your
less resilient self. You are holding this idea of yourself
more closely than the truth. The truth of you is who you
are now.

....

There are times you did not hit your note . . . But this
is not who you are. It bothers you *because* it is not who
you are.

....

Forgiveness isn't a way of getting off the hook. It's a way of
getting off the dime and moving forward in your life.

....

See yourself as the one who grew from the mistake, rather
than the one who made a mistake.

....

....

Your contribution is more productive than your regret.

....

It is not too late. It is not over. The world begins right now, if you wish.

15

Forgiving a Part of Yourself

THE PRACTICE: Sometimes we think we can't trust our-selves in the present because of "untrustworthy" decisions we made before. This is why we must forgive ourselves. We must see our past with compassion and in context. **Your practice is to look back at a past decision or situation that you feel bad about and reclaim yourself.** Think of it as a soul retrieval. Be willing to see why you did what you did and bless this choice.

For most of us, enlightenment isn't a sudden awakening, but a slow process of shining the light of consciousness onto those rejected, forgotten, and denied places within.
—TOKO-PA TURNER

The pain was there to show me how I had been thinking so much less of myself. The pain was not there to make me think even less of myself.
—TAMA KIEVES, from a journal entry

What if we could love *all* strands of our lives? Appreciate the *whole* song? I don't want to stay angry at parts of myself. I don't want to divorce them or lock them in a room far away from the main house. I don't want shame to weaken my own self-allegiance. I want to learn how to understand, respect, and love all of me. How about you?

At one point in my growth, I decided to forgive myself. I needed to let go of seeing myself as broken. I didn't want to have all these buried pockets of shame within me, "evidence" of my failure from past aspects of my life. I wanted to be present to my current life. I needed all of me here. **I knew I couldn't fully trust myself if I still believed I wasn't trustworthy.**

Of course, I understood that past mistakes led me to growth. I knew they were just mistakes. I knew the whole "you were doing the best you could at the time" line of thought. Or "If you really could have done it differently, you would have." I believed in these principles intellectually, but the words felt dry on my tongue. I had to get acceptance from my head to my suffering heart.

According to many religious and spiritual traditions, forgiveness is an absolute necessity. I'm a student and teacher of *A Course in Miracles,* and this deep work uses the term "forgiveness" in an unusual way. When *A Course in Miracles* talks about forgiveness, it means to see things differently. We are not looking to deny the events that happened. We are looking to change the meaning we gave to a behavior or outcome, a meaning that is creating unnecessary pain.

Here's the Evelyn Woods speed-reading version of this mind-bending process. We ask ourselves: *What am I making this mean?* Then we let go of the story or interpretation we have been telling ourselves. We become available to Spirit or the voice of love. A new story emerges. You are flooded with neutrality or compassion where before you felt pain.

The good news is that a miracle, or shift in perception, will take place instantaneously. The less-than-fun news is that it can take years for us to develop our readiness. It's worth every second.

SEEING YOUR STORY WITH NEW EYES

Sometimes it's hard to see our own behaviors from a different perspective. I have my own way of stepping back from my story. I use active imagination. I pretend I'm a cultural anthropologist in the field. I'm examining the behavior of a person in a culture I know nothing about.

*I don't want to stay angry at
parts of myself.*

I drop my opinions. I am curious. I hope to understand and learn about this person. I want to buy her a cup of coffee, though of course this is probably very bad anthropologist behavior.

Without judgment, I witness this person in *her* context, her way of seeing the world with the resources she had available at the time. I am eager to uncover the logic, hope, or even love in her decisions. I'm a bit like Captain Kirk wielding Star Trek's awesome prime directive: I will not impose my values. **I will not judge what was possible in the past based on any capabilities I might now have.**

I will tell you a very personal story, a story that always made me cringe. A story I never wanted to remember, much less examine. A story I now see differently. I'm so very grateful I looked back on my life with the restorative tool of awareness.

Much of this story comes straight from my journal. So, though it's written to myself and to the person involved, I hope it inspires you to reflect on an aspect of your past or present with new love and understanding.

Okay, here goes.

I don't have many regrets in my life. But this is one. I wish I had asked you the question I had on my mind. I wish I was *that* woman, bold, forthright, and courageous.

You had come home from your travels. "Travels" is a nice word. "Adventure" was the euphemism you used, or probably even "spiritual adventure." I would have said you came home from your druggy, grungy escape, and your abandonment of me, and every responsibility in your life.

While you traveled, you wrote me letters without return addresses, just a bird drawn in the corner in place of a post office box or residence. Once you wrote from a small beach in Oregon, where you sat all day and watched the Pacific Ocean until the sun set. I envied you. I was still in awe of you. "Observing one whole day" sounded powerful. You made everything sound powerful.

But you had ditched leases, child support, debts, and personal promises. You walked out of our seven-year relationship, in the middle of a conversation. You traipsed around the country and called your time "adventures in consciousness." I was having an adventure in consciousness, too, one I hadn't asked for. I was trying to navigate bone-crushing grief. I was trying to recover from rejection and the end of our world.

You broke up with me because you wanted freedom and, initially, to move in with another woman. You knew you needed freedom, though you said you didn't know what it would look like. You'd picked a tarot card. You'd read a passage in a Carlos Castaneda book. Hell, maybe you'd even gotten a fortune cookie or a feather from a pigeon lying in the grass at a forty-degree angle. It was all so meaningful. Your choices were always ordained. They were never your responsibility.

Then one day, you just came home. For a year or more, I'd secretly wished every godforsaken, ugly, sad day that I could be back together with you, even though I knew that wasn't a good idea. It wasn't something that would or should happen.

It was like saying, "This time I'll just do heroin on weekends." You know you are talking about a vortex that will erode your values and priorities. Still you wheedle. You idealize the needle.

I met you at Dietrich's coffee house on the corner. It was a pretty spring day and we walked to Cheeseman Park. We leaned against a tree you called Grandfather. I can't remember the details because the memory is gauzy and surreal. Even at the time, I knew that something big was happening. Something like the plot twist of the movie. I only remember this. I wish I had asked you what I wanted to ask you.

You were talking differently now. You were sounding like there were possibilities. "I think I'm ready now. I think I'm ready for us again." You said something like that. It may not have been as direct. It may have been like a bird song warbled with a hint, tinged with a message you knew that I would pick up on and understand.

I felt this hope. A little excitement. I felt this crash of sadness too, like a thud, a piano falling from a rooftop. I felt sick, a weird inner nausea. I felt like a door was open and the breeze was otherworldly cold. I wanted to ask. I wanted to ask you directly, "What do you mean? What do you mean, exactly?" I wanted to ask you, "Do you want to get back together now?"

But I couldn't.

I didn't.

I felt like I already knew the answer in my gut. I knew this was a dying bird. Maybe I just couldn't bear the answer. Or couldn't bear to hear you say something slithery again.

Couldn't bear to hear you say no, in a way that sounded like yes—and maybe—and a thousand worlds in between.

I felt like I knew the answer, maybe an answer you didn't even know. I felt like you were a ghost or an illusion, and this wasn't a real proposition. Deep within I knew that if it were real, it would have to be asked differently. Not like a jaunt. But like something that took into account everything that had gone on before. You would own your responsibility. You would have been willing to clean up all the broken glass with me.

No, you weren't saying it like that. You weren't acknowledging that there had a been a car wreck in our bedroom, living room, and life. You were saying it like, "Hey, maybe we could have a picnic—and I'll bring the popcorn." I knew inside myself that someone who was real about coming back after all we had been through wasn't going to start with a picnic.

There was a time I did ask you for definition. It was before you took off traveling. You had left our relationship for another woman, but we were friends-ish. Then we started getting together more often in the old house I lived in. We would talk and laugh and share just like we always had. We wouldn't make love, but we would talk about our love, our connection as big as the low hanging moon.

I'd asked you outright then, "Hey, where are we going with this?" Or maybe I even said, "Do you think we should get back together?" I remember your answer then. "Let's just stay in the present," you said.

I remember this answer, because it was a reckoning for me. Something snapped. Finally, a dragon reared up in me and said, "No way Jose, oh, and namaste." That was the start of me really beginning to move on. Your answer helped me.

Because I wouldn't stay in the present moment. I wasn't going to hang out there, after seven years of an intimate relationship, of you moving on to another woman, of me still talking to you because you felt shaken and missed me, missed us.

With someone else, or in the beginning of a relationship, that answer could have made sense. But with you, and the history we already shared, I knew what that floaty answer meant. There was no future. You weren't coming back or moving forward. You wanted this twilight zone. This Jell-O-like ground, a shifting landscape where anything could happen, but nothing serious would.

There would be no responsibility or reliability, only possibility. It was your comfort zone: have your cake, eat it too, date another cake, and philosophize like a guru. You could make the lack of clarity sound Zen-like and superior, and my hunger for specificity sound desperate or attached to an outcome. You were born for this kind of in-between limbo life. Finally, I came to see that I was not.

But that day in the park, you were suggesting we could or should get back together. You seemed sheepish. Half-hopeful. Yet something didn't feel right, even beyond the fact that it would have been crazy for us to get back together. I might have been open to that kind of crazy. Yet this felt hollow. I needed it to feel ragged and real. I didn't know this consciously. But I think unconsciously I knew you were just testing the waters. Maybe rolling the dice because you had no other possibilities. You were out of cards.

So I didn't ask the question. Part of me was afraid to hear no, to face rejection again. Only now I realize it wasn't only that. I was starting a tenuous new life. And part of me rose up like a mother bear, protecting her cub from a predator. You were dangerous. Always dangerous.

I had just started to find some solid ground. My world wasn't sexy. It wasn't transcendental. Yet it was real. And something about you that day was even more amorphous than your usual chameleon nature.

I have always wished I'd asked. Because then you would have closed the door definitively. Yet I see now that I did the best thing I could in a situation rigged with emotional trip-wires.

I did what I could. I think at the time I was still in shock. I didn't have my full faculties. I also know I knew the answer. *I knew what I knew.* Maybe I didn't need to hear the words from you.

Besides, I felt guarded. I knew I was still too enmeshed and vulnerable. Your words could have enlisted me. The mother bear in me sensed this susceptibility. So instinctively I didn't ask because you don't ask a traveling salesman to hear the pitch if you know you absolutely should not buy—especially when you're self-aware enough to know you'd buy everything, pay in full, and sign your life away.

I knew you could conjure up a fairy tale and I would beg for the starring role. So, I didn't invite the damage. Didn't ask for details. I let the moment pass. I didn't ask the question.

For years, I avoided thinking about that day in the park. I'd wince and stuff the memory back down. I felt bad about myself. I felt like I should have demanded a confrontation. Oh, I beat myself up over this.

I'd been telling myself this story: You have no backbone. Other women would have been bold. They wouldn't have even met him in the park. They certainly wouldn't have let him dangle vague invitations before them. You were weak. You never called him out.

These many years later, I am telling a new story. I was broken-hearted, barely coming back to life. Not asking the question wasn't a failure of courage. It was an attempt at discernment. *I was hurt-ing so much.* I couldn't see things as clearly as I would later. But I knew that I was afraid of him. I was afraid he'd say no, he didn't want to be with me. I was afraid of the trauma of new rejection. I had just begun to heal.

And I was afraid he'd say yes, or maybe. I knew I wasn't strong enough yet to resist his promises. Sure, I didn't stand up to him or call him out, as years later I wished I'd done. Yet I had done the right thing.

I didn't invite his promises into the light. I didn't get in the taxi with possibilities and half-truths. I let them pass by. I may not have definitively pushed him out of my life. But at least I didn't let him in. That was victory. I left the park intact that day, with no further drama. I moved on with my life.

I bless that young woman who got me here. She did the best she could then, so I can do the best I can now. I am no longer embarrassed by this part of myself. I am in awe of her. I owe her the life I have now.

SELF-TRUST INQUIRY

Is there a story in your life where you have made yourself wrong? If that part of you was doing the best it could, how do you imagine it would tell its story of what was going on?

SELF-TRUST-ISMS

Forgiving a Part of Yourself

Look back at a past decision . . . that you feel bad about and reclaim yourself. Think of it as a soul retrieval.

....

I knew I couldn't fully trust myself if I still believed I wasn't trustworthy.

....

Be willing to see why you did what you did and bless this choice.

....

I don't want to stay angry at parts of myself. I don't want to divorce them or lock them in a room far away.

....

I don't want shame to weaken my self-allegiance. I want to learn how to understand, respect, and love all of me.

....

I don't judge what was possible in the past based on any capabilities I might now have.

16

When You're Ridiculously Stuck in a Pattern

THE PRACTICE: Maybe you feel stuck in the same limitation again and again. The pattern is here to help you let go of this pattern—to help you shift the beliefs you have that create the pattern. Step onto holy ground. Be willing to see yourself differently. **Your practice is to stop looking at where you're lacking and start looking at the greatness in yourself that will attract great experiences.** Your strength is a magnet. When you start appreciating yourself more, you stop inviting limiting events and people.

*What if I can't change yet? I can notice and "name" what's going on. I don't have to shame myself. A fruit ripens in its own time.
I know progress will come from self-honesty.
Not from self-judgment.*
—TAMA KIEVES, from a journal entry

Your mistake does not define who you are . . .
you are your possibilities.
—OPRAH WINFREY

Sometimes you find yourself in a pattern that loops and repeats again and again. It's easy to get discouraged. Or to think you will always be stuck or thwarted, like a character in a Greek myth rolling a rock uphill, only to have it come rolling back down every single time until you think, *Please, just eat my liver out of my back and let's get this over with.*

If you're in that loop, please be gentle with yourself. You are taking on a significant healing. I'd say you're near the mother lode of blockage or misunderstanding about your worth. Congratulations. Because you're about to change your life like nothing else. Consider this from *A Course in Miracles*: "Trials are but lessons that you failed to learn presented once again, so where you made a faulty choice before you now can make a better one, and thus escape all pain that what you chose before has brought to you."

This is how the loop works. The inner story or illusion tricks you into believing that you are always going to be in the same place. Yet you are *never* in the same place. The pattern is the same. *But you are not the same.* You have new perspective and increased awareness each time. You make new micro choices. And that's the point. The pattern is here to help you change the pattern.

If you're stuck in one of these pattern loops, you've encountered your wormhole. Think Star Trek and the funky time-space-continuum irregularities that can help you do unusual things. You're about to change the nature of reality as you know it. Welcome to the adventure of expansion.

STEP ONTO HOLY GROUND

For several years, I couldn't find the help I needed for my business. I needed an awesome assistant. This didn't seem like it should be so hard. Normal people hired other people every day of the week. But I kept having abysmal experiences. You wouldn't even believe them if I told you. It is not an exaggeration to say I practically worked my way through the mood disorders section of the *DSM*, the psychiatric bible for mental disorders. Soon, I approached hiring with sadness. Okay, dread. Like nothing I did would matter. I would never, ever get what I needed.

Yes, at times, I'd get my hopes up. I'd find someone good, but then she decided to join a cult, start her own business, or go back to a high-paying, though flesh-eating, corporate IT job. I felt like I was at some amusement park game where a big hammer came out and smashed any white plate I put down. I no longer had faith in the possibility of new plates. I had faith in the smash.

I just couldn't see how my pattern would ever change. I tried hiring from Upwork. I tried hiring a company that helps you hire. I tried hiring from the recommendations of friends and word of mouth. I tried incantations, meditations, rewriting my ad, burning candles in my office, involving my community and more. Nothing panned out. I was in a *Groundhog Day*–type movie, the French arthouse tragedy version—where it always rains, there's no cheeky romance, and nothing moves forward except maybe the main character develops a facial tic or aneurysm. The credits roll.

One night, I poured my heart out to my artist friend Corinne. I was staying at her place, immersed in her spell of mosaics, paintings, feathers, and images everywhere. In bed that night, I kept thinking about my situation. Then suddenly this strange energy started running through me. *Take off your shoes and stand on holy ground,* said my inner voice. I wrote it in my journal. Suddenly an image popped into my mind. It was a portrait of my disappointment, a snapshot of how I felt when I approached each situation in this pattern.

The pattern is here to help you change the pattern.

I see this woman walking in trailing a train of ratty netting, empty cans, debris, old fish heads, rattling metal rusted keys that unlock doors of houses that have been demolished, torn paper, letters never sent and those that were thrown away in anger, old phone numbers, the people you never called, and the ones you did. The train goes on forever, clattering as I walk into the room. "I'm available," I say. "I'm open to something new and good."

But really, I have all this *mishigas*, this crazy accumulation of half sorrows and broken promises, and I'm inviting you to dance with all of this. Of course, I wonder why only the fishy characters show up, smelling of their own decay. Only complicated, worn-thin souls with histories of incompetency and frustration show up to dance with me.

Ahh . . . I realize. I must let go of this story, this long cape of sorrow, this train of misery. I need to come clean. I need to be innocent again, instead of feeling permeated with secret dread. It's time to find peace of mind with all that has come before. Because I don't want to stay blocked. I yearn to experience cosmic flow, excellent people, and grace.

I want to be available, *really available* to good. I want to feel as though anything can happen now—because I don't have anything from the past plunging me into a vibration of shame and failure.

Obviously, it's time to let go of the sludge of past disappointments. *But I don't know how to let go.*

I have an idea. I take a stab at it. I write out this prayer:

> *Spirit, I am asking now for you to help cleanse me.*
>
> *Help me release these memories, memories that are fashioned in a way that hurt me, stories of pain, stories told from a dark point of view, without the light beams of healing.*
>
> *Spirit, I know you have another way of seeing my past.*
>
> *Through your eyes it is holy. It is medicine. It is purposeful. It is all part of the truth, the Greater Story of me. There is intelligence in every aspect of my life. There is no place for shame.*
>
> *I am not what happened to me. I am not limited to only what has been true so far. And through your vision, I will even see that all that has occurred so far had strains of grace within it. I open to seeing with your eyes. I am willing to experience something new, something I've never experienced before.*
>
> *I ask to step onto holy ground. I am willing to remove my shoes and sweep away the dust from the past. I am willing to forgive myself. I am willing to forgive others. I ask for help.*

ACCEPTING RESPONSIBILITY. WHOA, IT'S NOT HAPPENING *TO ME*. IT'S HAPPENING *FOR ME*.

This was the biggest problem at the time: it's hard to "see things differently" because I only have evidence of what I already believed. How can I believe in something good when I believe things will fail, and I have ample evidence of being right?

At the time I felt like some strange Statue of Liberty saying, "Give me your broken, your twisted, those who can't do what they say they can. Bring me your defensive and fickle. Give them to me. I am worthy of them. I expect lack and injury. I expect to be disappointed. My heart is prepared to break."

Of course, I don't expect these things consciously. But I am in a pain spin. I am broken before I even start. When something undesirable happens, it feels familiar.

Why am I attracting these people? Friends say it's a numbers game with hiring. Maybe that's true, but I know it's more. Am I not paying enough? Is the ad written poorly? Is Mercury in retrograde forever now? Is it me? Did I torture some servant in a past life? Really, I want to scream—*What the hell?*

Then I remember something I heard the spiritual teacher Marianne Williamson say (long before she ran for president). A woman asked Marianne, "When I'm dating, how come I attract all these losers?" Marianne shot back, "The problem isn't that you're attracting rotten guys. The problem is that you give them your number."

Bam! Responsibility smacked me in the third eye. I am not innocent. *I give them my number.* For me this meant I give someone a chance, someone who disappoints me from the start. I don't trust my instincts and run. I might sense that this is going skunky, but I think, *I'll make it work.* I can be a Cirque du Soleil acrobat and twist and hang by a thread. *I am flexible,* I tell myself with pride. But over time I realize I have no pride.

When friends push me to let go of someone who isn't right, I realize I don't believe in abundance. I don't believe there will be "other fish in the sea." I don't trust that I will have what I need, so I hang on to what isn't giving me what I need.

Of course, I wanted to trust life on a deeper level. I needed to imagine that I could have better experiences.

Finally, I came to this realization: **You need to see yourself differently to have different possibilities.** This is the miracle and the invitation.

FORGIVING MYSELF FOR BEING WHERE I WAS

I had to forgive myself. Deep down, a part of me believed I deserved bad things.

What about you? I urge you to drop your shame. Maybe you have been "playing small." Maybe you're irresponsible. Cheap. Sneaky. Passive-aggressive. *Whatever.* It doesn't matter. You can begin to heal and rise right now.

You deserve good love. Do not let a false sense of guilt make you think you deserve subpar moldy garbage all your life. Life is not punishing you. You are punishing yourself.

It's only pain that makes us make limited and unskillful choices.

In my healing around hiring, I got honest with myself about what made me feel inadequate. First there was money. I worried that I couldn't pay top dollar. I wasn't Google or a law firm.

Yet I remembered what another entrepreneur suggested. "You need to look at the other benefits and 'currency' you offer." I offered a lot: Flexibility. Meaningful work. Laughter. Joy. Stability. Plus the pay would increase as we grew.

Then another thought landed in my intuitive inbox. *With the right people, it would all work somehow. We would work out what needed to work out.* Self-forgiveness was already working its radiant voodoo.

I kept thinking I had to be perfect in order to be able to ask for things. I didn't realize I was already the perfect opportunity for the right people. I didn't have to wait.

So I tackled another insecurity. "Well, what if I'm a micromanager?" I asked one of my friends. My friend chewed her lip. "Okay, what if you do have a control-freak streak?" She continued, "Maybe you own that you care about your work because you're a powerhouse . . . but you're also willing to look at any part of that that isn't healthy. Meanwhile, can you forgive yourself for not fully trusting after you've been let down?" *What? I could be flawed—and not damned?*

Of course, I could grow. Like everyone else on the planet, I would do better in an environment of love. But I had hired others who had judged me for "wanting too much," often to justify their mistakes. I came to believe I was asking too much, so I didn't ask enough.

Now I knew that I wanted to create working relationships that were generous and flowed both ways. I'm always going to support the highest potential of others. I will always open the doors of possibility. The difference was that now I would be a doorway, not a doormat. I deserved an equal exchange of energy, a match. But I wanted a match of my strength, not of my low self-esteem.

Then my world got even bigger. My friend Marney, a consultant in my business, challenged me one day. "You're always willing to work with others and help them grow. What if you were working with someone who could help you grow? What if you could work together and become your best selves and get kick-ass work done?" *Oh, don't be telling me about Shangri-La now, woman,* I wanted to say. Still, I wondered. Somewhere deep within a light turned on.

"You're a great boss," she continued, and yes, Marney is a great friend. But she rattled off tangible examples so that I'd listen. "Sister, you're patient and encouraging. You never fly off the handle, even when the flan hits the pan." Her litany of positive feedback worked like a spell. It slipped past my resistance. *Of course I deserved love. Of course I deserved goodness.* We all do. But finally, *I* did.

Sure, I had stumbled in some things, but I hit it out of the ballpark in other areas. I realized, then, that I'd been looking at where I wasn't amazing, instead of looking at where I was.

I wasn't a piece of work. I was a work in progress.

I didn't have to be right for everyone. I just had to be right for my people.

For years, I've taught other artists, leaders, and visionaries how to find their right clients and opportunities. I've always said, "You will have your people. There is an intelligent order in the Universe. You will have your people." But at last, *at long last,* I began to believe this was true in hiring too. Even for me.

Here's the door-opener, the crystal key. **When you want to attract great people to you, you need to remember the greatness within yourself.**

SEEING YOURSELF THROUGH LOVE'S EYES

One day you may see yourself in your strength, and you will remember who you are.

I had been guiding one of my five-day immersive retreats. I was in my element, pure flow. It's this truth I trust when teaching. I will know what to say. The room will know what to say. The energy will have its way.

Sitting at a lunch of organic greens and fresh multigrain bread, I talked to Rebekkah, one of my favorite retreatants. I told her about my struggle with my assistant at that time, the person I had who not only didn't do her job well, but who was grumpy, blaming, and incredibly lazy unless it involved defending herself in which case the woman had the fury of a bull and the dedication of a monk. I knew the passive-aggressive, defensive one had been a bad hire, but I felt stuck. I prattled on with all my usual reasons.

Rebekkah looked at me with deep brown, intelligent eyes. "I want more for you," she said. I felt this cosmic transmission, and any diminished self-image I had melted. I witnessed myself through *her* eyes. I was this semi-brilliant savant facilitator taking everyone else to the heights of their capabilities and greatest potential. Of course I deserved a competent assistant.

I saw that I was doing my right work and it was stirring waves of love and change in the world. This wasn't my ego talking. This was my ego *not* talking, not taking down the truth of the work. I was helping maverick souls breathe, end their own absenteeism, believe in their dreams, and embody their true potential. I was living my calling. This calling required support. I was just a part of a universal plan. It made sense to me that there would be someone for me in that plan.

It was like waking up out of a trance. It *was* waking up out of a trance. I suddenly *knew* that I deserved great help and support. It wasn't a belief I needed to affirm. The knowing was just there like a bowl of green Granny Smith apples.

You don't need to know how to empower yourself. In the right moment, infinite grace empowers you.

You might get this love from a therapist or coach. Or your best friend, rabbi, or a line in a book or song. It will come from the Wonder Department of Higher Powers through whatever channel is necessary to reach you. It will come. Yes, you will think it's never going to happen. But it will.

Remember, your pattern, whatever it is, is here for this reason. **The pattern is here to help you let go of this pattern. You are meant to forgive yourself.** You are meant to let go of all the sad stories you have made up about yourself. You are meant to step into the light and live your right life.

The assistant I had had an issue with resigned shortly after my epiphany with Rebekkah. Soon thereafter, I hired someone I love to the moon and back. Having found someone so amazing,

I believed in humanity again. There are always good people. Miracles abound. They arrive when we choose to love ourselves more.

IT'S ALL ABOUT SELF-LOVE

I realized now that many of my previous hires or candidates had been sent as messengers. They were showing me what I believed about myself. I don't know that I would have seen my self-attack otherwise.

I would have told you I had great self-esteem, but my ongoing hiring situation helped my unconscious beliefs become conscious. They exposed my deeper conversations with myself. I can see now that this had never really been about hiring. It had always been about learning to love and respect myself more.

Every single issue in life comes down to the same thing. How much do I love, trust, and believe in myself? Because I will act accordingly. And the unfoldment of my life will reflect my choices.

SELF-TRUST INQUIRY

What would taking responsibility for your part
in the pattern look like for you?
How is your pattern helping you to love yourself more?

SELF-TRUST-ISMS

When You're Ridiculously Stuck in a Pattern

The inner story or illusion tricks you into believing that you are always going to be in the same place. Yet you are *never* in the same place.

The pattern is here to help you change the pattern.

I want to be available, *really available* to good. I want to feel as though anything can happen now.

I kept thinking I had to be perfect in order to be able to ask for things. I didn't realize I was already the perfect opportunity for the right people.

Life is not punishing you. You are punishing yourself.

When you want to attract great people to you, you need to remember the greatness within yourself.

17

The Power of an Open Heart

THE PRACTICE: Forgiveness always sets your power free. Because love is your power. And judgment blocks your love. You may be judging someone else's choices based on what you think is right or what you think they could do. But you do not know the full story. **Your practice is to remind yourself that it is not that you should not judge, but that you cannot judge.** Keeping your heart open allows you to connect with yourself.

If you judge people,
you have no time to love them.
—MOTHER TERESA

Everything that irritates us about others can
lead us to an understanding of ourselves.
—CARL JUNG

I have no idea who judged who first. But I know I wanted a different mother at times. And I know she yearned for a different daughter, though she might never have said it. Judgment kept us from witnessing each other's light. But *A Course in Miracles* shares: "It's not that you should not judge, but that you cannot judge." Slowly, I'm beginning to grasp how muddled my mind is with ideas about what others should do that might not even be true. But I do know this: **Judgment blocks love. And love is all I want.**

This is one of the ways I felt judged by my mother: she'd gaze at a young woman swaddling a baby in the mall. "Don't you want one of those?" she'd ask. *Again with this.* Like maybe I'd changed my mind or my internal organs. I didn't want a child—which my mother knew from our last 453 debates about this topic. But *she* wanted me to be a mother. She wanted to be a grandmother. Basically, she wanted me to want what she wanted.

Why can't she love *me*? I am not the prototype she'd hoped for. She wants the "nice daughter" edition who would skip down the aisle with a rich guy and have a baby. She does not want a daughter who is "in transition," and seeks emotional support—so not in her playbook. She doesn't need a daughter who wants to change the world. She wants a daughter who wants to change a diaper.

Shopping at the mall, my mother starts again with the kid thing. I choke back tears. Then I attack back, sly like a cougar. I start talking about *other people*. "You know, it's so superficial to think you can find meaning at Macy's. It's only people without purpose that need to shop all the time. I feel sorry for them."

I lecture as though I am the world's leading authority on something. Meanwhile, I know full well that my mother shopped because she was lonely. She didn't have much to do. She didn't socialize, have hobbies, causes, or, let's just say it, *grandchildren*. She loved the diversion of looking at new outfits and jewelry on sale. She talked to young women at the perfume counters. "I enjoy being a Goyl," she'd sing out loud to them. I think it was her rendition of an Ethel Merman song.

Here's how I judged my mother: I wanted a mother who would *see me*. A mother who celebrated my daring and encouraged me to chase my dreams across the Universe, if that's the small price it required.

I also wanted my mother to be less superficial. I wanted a mother who might read to the blind, take up pottery, research Mayan spirituality, recycle, garden, or help a neighbor, a third-world country, or a stray dog. But my mother watched crime dramas and Hallmark movies on television, played solitaire, read romance novels, and shopped. That's pretty much it.

I judged my mother with the white-hot heart of a very young woman. I wanted so much more of life for her . . . and I wanted more from her. Intensity and possibility surged through my young bright bones. I had all my roads ahead of me. I wasn't tired yet.

It was easy to judge my mother. It was also inexperienced of me to do so.

My mother didn't appreciate self-improvement. She craved a plump cushion. "I'm lazy," she'd tell me. I couldn't understand, but Paul, my partner, once said to me, "Maybe this is her lifetime to rest. Who knows what she has gone through in this life or in any others?" My partner, the wonder soul, who always gives everyone a pass.

My mother did have a rough past. She lost her father when she was an eight-year-old girl with skinny legs and buckteeth. A few years later, her new stepfather stabbed himself. Finally, she married my father, a man who called her stupid in front of her children and pulled the tubes out of the television set so she couldn't watch her shows. So, yes, maybe she just wanted a little comfort. Maybe she wasn't up for saving the pandas. Maybe she just wanted to look at beautiful things in stores where no one yelled at her.

WHAT IF CIRCUMSTANCES ARE NEUTRAL—AND ONLY HAVE THE MEANING YOU GIVE THEM?

I used to think that just watching television wasn't living. I see now that television was my mother's best friend. It gave her a ticket into others' lives. Hallmark and HBO showed up nightly in my mother's condo and provided intimacy and escape.

Hallmark movies gave my mother the sweet, safe family her eight-year-old heart dreamed of. Other channels let her experience a steamy romance and finally be desired, while she, still with bucked teeth, ate her microwaved kettle popcorn in the dark. I'm grateful for these consistent friends and alchemists that showed up in the guise of entertainment. I'm grateful that my mother experienced hours of delight.

One night, wandering through Macy's on a Friday evening, checking out the sales rack of earrings, I thought of my mother. I often do when I shop. She comes to me unbidden. In grocery stores too, the canned soup aisle and frozen foods section.

She died in a car accident years ago. I have never totally allowed this fact in. I just tell myself we are having an even more long-distance relationship than before. These days, when I think of her, it's as though she floods me. The love floods me. The love, love, love of her, for her, and from her.

On this particular evening, I was looking at a pair of silver and purple earrings I really didn't need. I was tired. I was lonely. That Friday night I was sinking into the swamp of failure and grief because of stupid self-comparison and a plan that hadn't come through.

I felt numb. Like a bug turned on its back, thrashing slowly, losing interest. So I was chasing amusement in silver dangle earrings and trying on samples of perfumes and skin creams. The department store was quiet. The Clinique esthetician looked bored. So did the young girl grouping the tan handbags in the new spring collection. It felt like the temple of the bored.

I was bored too, bored with the repetitive rants within about how I should be living my life, the constant race against time, all I wanted to experience, and the disappointment I felt in this moment.

Judgment blocks love.
And love is all I want.

Then I thought of my mother. The tears came. I began to cry as I remembered an earlier time in my life, berating my mother, making fun of her, trying to shame her.

Suddenly, I blessed every single pair of earrings that had ever twinkled for my mother. I blessed every saleswoman anywhere that had laughed with my mother. I blessed the stores in the malls for their background music harmless as grape soda, their safe ambience, their makeshift shelter from the ugly, demanding encroachments of life, and the distractions they offer from pain.

Yes, I have judged American consumerism. The pursuit of more, the waste and packaging that fill the landfills. I know that distraction isn't an answer for your life. But I also know that life is a bundle of contradictions. That distraction from pain can sometimes be medicine and a mercy. Catching your breath is catching your breath. Sure, maybe we should meditate or run. But sanctuary is sanctuary.

That night in Macy's, I allowed this unexpected wave of forgiveness to overtake me. I know I'm on the right path when I see everything with love.

I forgive my mother and I forgive the mall and I forgive myself and I forgive all of us who are stumbling at times or not yet reaching the height of what is possible for us. Suddenly, I saw the Poughkeepsie Mall as a temple or tabernacle, a refuge where my mother could ease heartache and alienation.

There she would encounter the benign community of others. She would find rack after rack of beauty. Hope, in its flowing white gown, would walk beside her gently murmuring, *Look at that pretty thing, look at that one.* Because with each new bracelet or diamond-cut sapphire-like stone, there was a new rush or a chance that life could shimmer.

Who am I to say that an amulet or a mala bead is more meaningful than an opal ring or a beaded, braided bracelet? For me, God isn't so much a man in the sky or even the emptiness in a Zendo. It's the feeling of being loved or safe. It's the feeling of no longer being alone and slipping past self-judgment and isolation.

I think Jesus, Buddha, Yahweh, or Allah might say to find your contentment in a higher love or acts of service. But I also think that every one of those dudes would have laughed with delight as my mother tried on a necklace and sang, "I feel pretty, I feel pretty." I think each one of them would have wanted her soul to feel free and soothed. I don't believe in a spirituality that judges. I believe in a spirituality that frees. It's love that leads us to love.

My mother once told me that I was the person who had loved her most in life. I cherish these words like a slab of gold.

It's so easy to judge others from our point of view. Maybe love is relinquishing our point of view and glimpsing the world from someone else's eyes. Forgiveness comes naturally, then.

SELF-TRUST INQUIRY

Who have you been judging?
Can you imagine the world from their point of view?

SELF-TRUST-ISMS

The Power of an Open Heart

It's not that you should not judge, but that you cannot judge.

Judgment blocks love. And love is all I want.

It was easy to judge my mother. It was also inexperienced of me to do so.

For me, God isn't so much a man in the sky . . . It's the feeling of being loved or safe.

I don't believe in a spirituality that judges. I believe in a spirituality that frees. It's love that leads us to love.

Maybe love is relinquishing our point of view and glimpsing the world from their eyes. Forgiveness comes naturally, then.

KICKSTARTS AND PRACTICES

Have at it. Play with these. Trust yourself. Go where you're guided . . .

Pick Three Self-Trust-isms from Part IV. Journal about them. Maybe make some art. Meditate or reflect on the words that spoke to you. Discuss them with someone else. Let these chosen phrases unlock a new awareness and conversation within.

1. **The Pattern Intervention.** Where do you feel stuck? What old ideas do you need to stop dragging in? Imagine a wise voice says to you, "Step onto holy ground. Anything is possible." Journal "If I was beginning again, I would . . ."

2. **Forgiveness Inventory.** Write a list of perceived failures that you are willing to transform. What images of yourself do you need to release? Describe who you would be without this list.

3. **Role Reversal Writing.** Think about someone you are judging. Now write to yourself from their point of view, explaining their pain, desires, and personal story.

4. **Play Cultural Anthropologist.** Write a dialogue between a curious, emotionally neutral interviewer and a part of you that did something you wish to forgive. Let your anthropologist ask questions. Seek to understand, not to judge.

5. **Ritual of Release.** Design your own ritual for symbolically letting go of an event in the past. You might write the lessons you learned from the event. You may want to cast something symbolic into a body of water, bury it in dirt, or burn it.

6. **Write Yourself a Letter of Forgiveness.** Where have you been judging yourself or making yourself wrong? Write a letter of apology and encouragement to yourself.

PART V

From Self-Neglect to Self-Care

YOUR WILD WELL-BEING AWAITS

THE BLOCK: Self-Neglect

THE BREAKTHROUGH: *Self-Care*

YOU GET IN YOUR OWN WAY
by neglecting what you need.

YOU DISCOVER YOUR OWN WAY
when you practice self-care.

~

You may not trust yourself because you are neglecting yourself. Subsisting on fumes. Being "productive," even when it's not productive. Ignoring smoke signals from within. You may think boundaries are self-centered, instead of centered in Self.

Yet know this: you cannot be an automaton and a force of white lightning at the same time. Old habits yield old results. Societal norms isolate you from your own wild well-being.

But what if your exceptional life requires devotion? The way you treat yourself is your prayer. You will trust yourself when you practice self-care.

We experience quantum leaps when we start attending to our depths. Dare self-compassion. Rest. Say no to being carelessly busy. Say yes to being intentional.

In this section we will look at the revolutionary habits that ignite a revolutionary life.

18

Becoming a Self-Compassionate Witness

THE PRACTICE: On any given day, you may be listening to an inner narrator that is criticizing you. Self-care requires that you see your life—and yourself—through the eyes of grace instead of judgment. **Your practice is to observe your life through the eyes of a radically encouraging advisor or Spirit.** Focus on what you can appreciate and respect about yourself in any situation that is causing you stress. Choose the power of self-compassion over the diminishment of self-criticism.

You have every right to desire progress. But it's disabling to condemn where you are. Thriving comes from loving, not from withholding love.
—TAMA KIEVES, from *Thriving Through Uncertainty*

The more you praise and celebrate your life,
the more there is in life to celebrate.
—OPRAH WINFREY

Self-care has finally made it into the mainstream vernacular which means now we have apps and longer to-do lists. Best of all, we have a new reason to harass ourselves. I see a lot of people *stressing* about not getting to yoga or picking up their supplements, and I can't help but feel as though we are losing sight of the velvet bull's-eye.

You can drink celery juice or kombucha. Bathe in lavender-bliss-scented water. Listen to your Insight Timer app to get eight hours of sleep, and run three times a week in shoes that cost more than your car payment. My opinion, though, is that nothing makes nearly as much of a difference as how we see and treat ourselves.

Let's be real. You can be criticizing the hell out of yourself even in pricey bathwater. You can squash your grief or hopes until you feel like the gray slush at the side of a road, and really, I don't know how much wheatgrass is going to help with that.

That's why I'm going to suggest that self-compassion move to the top of your self-care list. I invite you to see your exact life with wild and abundant kindness. *There is so much good you can see about yourself and your life right now.* This one choice changes the axis of every decision you make or action you take. **The way you see—and treat—yourself within your life *is* your life.** Why climb to the top of a mountain if you are climbing in self-abandonment? Achievements without self-compassion taste like cardboard.

There is a Buddhist practice called witnessing. It's a process of looking at things and being neutral. Just noticing. *This brown leaf. This thumbtack. This email that says, "No, thank you, you didn't get the job and yes, you are defective."* Witnessing is a way of slowing down the mind and busting it out of the groove of autopilot and reactiveness.

I've taken that mindfulness practice and tricked it out a bit. I call my self-care weaponry "compassionate witnessing." My home-brewed technique has helped me turn an ordinary day riddled with self-judgment into a gospel choir of self-homage. I'll give you an example that might also change how you see any nagging un-finished things in your life.

Here's how you practice. Ignore the usual nitpicking narra-tor you hear in your mind. Instead, begin to observe your life from the point of view of a radically encouraging advisor, your Higher Self or someone who cares about you. Not someone who cares, as in, is afraid you will botch it up and miss *another* boat. Rather, someone who believes in your soul strength and wants you to recognize how well you're doing—right now. Here's what that advisor and I would like you to know: your life rocks. It's time to take it in.

SEEING THE MESS OF MY DESK (AND LIFE) DIFFERENTLY . . .

I am not a neat person. I'd say the organization of my desk is "early modern shipwreck," though some might use the word "shambles." I imagine Ms. Tidying Up, Marie Kondo, that sweet TV organiz-ing expert, crumpling before my desk. The camera cuts out. Her soft clicking Japanese encouragements turn into howls and whines of psychic pain. I am a badass of spillage.

There's a coffee mug stained with rings on the inside like the ages of a tree, a pizzazz-blue nail polish bottle, my calendar, three books, pads of paper with notes, magic markers, candles, a stray Advil, and more. Of course, there are also pillars and stacks of "important papers" that must be sorted but will remain undisturbed until they dissolve into dust—or I do.

When I'm feeling frustrated, I see my desk as a shrine to failure. The disarray represents all I haven't accomplished in my life. All that is unfinished. All that could be or would be but isn't. I see laziness, the failure to put away a pair of blue earrings or a copy of *The New Yorker*. I don't think these thoughts consciously. But I know that when I am not paying attention to my mindset, the jungle drums of self-attack thrum in the background.

> *The way you see—and treat—*
> *yourself within your life is your life.*

One afternoon, I caught myself beating myself up and I decided to practice compassionate witnessing. First, I acknowledge that I am seeing my desk and life in a way that makes me feel like an older dog who has had a number two–type "accident" on white carpeting. I am embarrassed by myself. I also feel overwhelmed. **So I begin by asking myself, how can I see this differently?** This is the mind-altering prayer of *A Course in Miracles*. It's a trumpet that parts the gates between the worlds and ushers in the hubba-hubba consciousness of all that is beautiful and true.

Suddenly I feel this other voice speak to me about my desk. Now, I am a little Jewish thing, but I swear I hear a gospel mama and she's wearing a hat the size of a panda cub. She stands up, giving testimony. She is done with my mind baloney. She says, "You got to praise the love here." Then she continues . . .

"Praise the desire. Praise the part of you that has desires. Praise the part of you that fails. Praise the optimist of dreams, ideas, and projects, and the hope that it will all get done, will all fall into place, with time like you got to spare. Praise the part of you that has this desire, this relentless, walloping desire to make progress, create, lose weight, fall in love, feed your family, write books, help the world, return phone calls, go to the doctor, do something about that hair, and organize yourself for tax season. Praise the desire. Praise the fire. This is Mount Vesuvius erupting with heat. Desire is the spitfire of creation. And you got to know that life-force doesn't give birth all pretty and neat.

"So pray you never get everything all wrapped up, because it's a holy joy to have things you want to do or change. Pray this river never runs dry. Let that river come from love. Don't let that river come from need or anger. Let that river come from love."

Now I begin to look at things differently. I look at them as a compassionate witness. I *appreciate* that I have an ambitious, rambunctious mind that collects ideas and possibilities like a crow builds its nest with shiny objects, twigs, straw, and stolen artifacts. An old earring here, a rusted beer bottle cap, a crumpled phone number. I love that I'm in the middle of reading three books at a time. I love that I have not one, but two different Ganesh statues on my desk and a bottle of herbal calming fragrance that my friend Grace shared with me when I visited her last. I love that I surround myself with things that feel good to me.

I LOVE THAT I'M IN PROCESS. I LOVE THAT I'M STILL BUILDING. I LOVE THAT I'M STILL HOPING.

I love that I still have dreams and plans and interests, despite setbacks, obstacles, and age. I am engaged in my life and that is holy. *I see that striving is a virtue.* Life isn't always about arriving. And the earrings? I bless the part of me that allowed me to do one less thing in my life. To be carefree. To be free of obligation when she felt tired. Now with new energy, thanks to this self-acceptance infusion, I put the earrings away. Look at that.

Self-love took a shrine to impotence and failure and turned it into a celebration for all the evidence of being alive and brimming with interest and possibility.

Finally, I use my compassionate witness tool to rise above myself further, to see myself in third person. I practice gazing at myself on this ordinary workday. Here's what I write:

> I've been given a one-way ticket as Tama Kieves, and I want to know her. I want to sit with her. I want to infuse her day with radical love. She is busy thinking about all the things she needs to do. I want to sit with her and stroke her hair. I want to celebrate her singular soul. I want her to slow down and revere her life as I do. I want to remind Tama that she is doing so much better than she ever sees. I'm so proud of her. She is showing up, best she can. *She is showing up. Over and over.* I want her to take in the radiance of this one day on earth in this one moment of being Tama—because it will never come again. And just this one moment, taking in the beingness of the one-of-a-kind life-force of Tama, is worth a whole lifetime.

I realize *I* want that abundance that comes from loving mindfulness too. Hell yes, I want that kind of active self-compassion. I want to be present for myself and living and breathing from this nourishment.

In fact, I want that kind of active self-compassion for all of us. Let us be rock stars of perspective.

SELF-TRUST INQUIRY

What part of yourself (or life) needs
more self-compassion right now?

What might a radically encouraging advisor, Spirit,
or someone who cares about you say to you about this situation?

~

SELF-TRUST-ISMS

Becoming a Self-Compassionate Witness

....

Self-care requires that you see your life—and yourself—
through the eyes of grace instead of judgment.

....

You can drink celery juice or kombucha. Bathe in lavender-
bliss-scented water . . . nothing makes nearly as much of a
difference as how we see ourselves.

....

Because let's be real. You can be criticizing the hell out of
yourself even in pricey bathwater.

....

The way you see—and treat—yourself within your life *is*
your life.

....

I invite you to see your exact life with wild and abundant
kindness . . . This one choice changes the axis of every decision you make or action you take.

....

There is so much good you can see about yourself and your
life right now.

19

Rest Gives You Wings

THE PRACTICE: if you want to be an eagle, get off the hamster wheel. You are keeping up with what is. Your exceptional life requires a break from ordinary doing. Quantum leaps depend on deepening yourself, not depleting yourself. **Your practice is to take space and rest so that you can regenerate, recalibrate, and become a conduit for your creativity and divine instincts.** A holy guided life requires space and time.

Take exquisite care of yourself and spontaneous strategies, synchronicities, and opportunities will match your inner abundance . . . This is not your father's productivity.
—TAMA KIEVES, from *A Year Without Fear*

Almost everything will work again if you unplug it for a few minutes, including you.
—ANNE LAMOTT

Will you trust your body and soul, or will you trust the dominant messaging of the culture? Just in case you're *actually* evaluating this, let me also add that we now have more documented sickness, anxiety, and depression than ever before. But hey, you don't need me to tell you that it sucks to keep pushing yourself when you're exhausted.

Here's what you might need me to tell you though. When you do not rest, you hold yourself back from expansion. Contrary to the hubris of popular behavior, you cannot run on fumes and grow into a metropolis of wonder. Everything you really want comes from feeling good inside yourself. Everything.

Taking rest is a private revolution. Rest is so obscenely not about forcing. To some of us, not taking action can seem so out of control. Yet not taking action can be an action that lifts you out of scarcity and into the land of milk and honey.

If you want to be an eagle,
you have to get off the hamster wheel.

Conscious rest is not just doing nothing. It's nourishing our neurochemistry, our nervous systems, and our souls. It's watering the seeds that you can't see. This is medicine. We need time to integrate, rejuvenate, and allow our deeper truth and creativity to germinate. You will see things differently. That's why a holy guided life requires space and time.

Let's keep it simple. Rest is a commitment to who you want to be.

THE CULTURAL NORM IS CRAY CRAY

We think of exhaustion as a badge of honor. Look how hard we're working. Look at the shadows and bags beneath our eyes. Just look at how much we have to do! *We are so important.*

We all laugh about how "bad" we are. We high-five the challenges and guzzle caffeine or rely on sugar like a lover. We may neglect our loved ones or the sensitive parts of ourselves who are frantically waving tattered bright red flags. Sometimes we get so out of balance, we don't even remember the life we're missing.

Think about it. Sleep deprivation is one of the tools the military uses to torture enemies and drive them to psychosis. I know there have been times when I've been so tired that I couldn't think straight. I accepted crap and thought it was a field of daisies on a silver platter. You probably have too.

Numbness shouldn't be a status symbol, but it is. I remember visiting a friend at my old law firm. Just then, Ellen, one of the senior litigation partners, bolted into the elevator in the lobby. "Ellen, how are you?" I called out. She smiled and waved. "Well, I'll live," she said, and the elevator door closed. It was funny. It was code: *I'm slammed. I'm tired. I'm a goddamn rock star.*

In my coaching practice, I've met a ton of Ellens and Toms as well. Putting out fires. Up to their eyeballs. Who had time to breathe or dream? Who could listen to the inner friend? One Ellen, an executive who had scaled the ranks of a software firm, told me about her life at the top. "I'm the bleary-eyed wizard behind the curtains," she said. "But hey, I have expensive toys."

Ellen sat alone in her big empty house drinking merlot at the granite counter in her kitchen. She had great faucets and a fridge the size of a rhinoceros, but she hadn't gazed at the moon in months. She was estranged from her daughter. Her cholesterol numbers kept rising. If she had a second to herself, she wanted to be numb.

It's hard to be available to our depths in a nonstop world. It's hard to calm down to the cello notes of self-awareness. Every morning we're stimulated through the media and internet: the icebergs are melting, there's been another mass shooting, the stock market fell, a new war broke out, and that bump on your elbow could definitely be a rare tumor—but if it isn't, don't worry, you probably have a tumor *somewhere*. Then your ex-husband's new babe posts pics on Facebook and, girl, she is skinnier and happier than you. Good morning!

AN EXCEPTIONAL LIFE REQUIRES MORE...
AND LESS

Maybe you think it's just the way things are, or this is what it takes to cope in everyday life. However, coping with insanity is not the crown of a spiritual life. Just coping can stunt us. We are here to rise.

Do you really want to keep the same circus going all the time? You may have to step away from the big tent. It may be your time to release trauma, conditioning, and patterns of constriction that conflict with the signature energy of your highest good. It could be time to feel whole again.

Respect your life. Choose to be a conduit of grace. Allow yourself to experience insights and energy that will expand your identity. You might be aching for this. The more you wish to do in this life, the more you need to regenerate and recalibrate.

Quantum leaps require deepening: quieting distractions and our everyday task mind. We slip out of one identity to open to a larger one. Self-care opens the doors to receptivity.

There's a difference between a Porsche and a Ford. The Porsche requires *more* maintenance because it *performs at another level*. You, however, may be treating yourself like a scrapyard moped and still insisting on taking the world by storm. Eventually your engine complains like an old peasant woman with tired feet. **You can only perform according to the level of care you receive.**

There are subtle messages informing you constantly. The voice of love within speaks to you all throughout the day. How can you attend to these instructions when your everyday mind is screeching on a loudspeaker, hustling you through an endless relay race of tasks? You may not hear your soul when your nervous system is bathed in cortisol. High alert is one frequency. Deep alert is another.

Space, time, and rest from the everyday mind is spiritual hygiene and homecoming.

Owning your brilliant connection to freedom starts from undoing, not doing. Most religions and spiritual traditions teach this principle of renewal. You must empty your rice bowl if you want to fill it with new rice, says Zen Buddhism. In Judaism, there is a Sabbath day every week, a day to stop ordinary tasks and await the divine. Christianity tells us to only pour new wine into new wineskins, not the saggy, tired old whining mind that needs a glass of wine. I may be paraphrasing here.

There is a doing that can only happen when we *take time to be* and *stop doing* everything that gets in the way of beckoning wonder and healing.

HOW YOU TREAT YOURSELF IS YOUR PRAYER

I didn't know that nurturing myself was a divine act of grace. I didn't know that sometimes the body ruled the mind. I didn't know I couldn't connect to my soul because I was tired, beaten up, and psychologically gut punched. I didn't know that rest would signal the angels. Or that I had to take care of myself in order to hear the voice of deep wisdom or impeccable guidance. Who knew that feeling like crap would not induce the music of the spheres?

I want to tell you about an unusual experience I had that made me believe that resting may just be the first step to self-love, certainty, and secret-agent capacities. I traveled early to the North Carolina retreat center in the mountains because I wanted to take care of myself before leading a weekend retreat there. I thought I'd want to spin around the grounds, do a yoga class, check out some spiritual bling at the gift shop, or catch up on reading about a thousand books.

Once there, I just stopped. I didn't want to do anything. Everything was so quiet. I felt compelled to rest. I lay down on the single white bed, and I swear it was made of clouds and generosity. I could feel my nervous system oozing into a state of honey.

It sounds silly to say that I had a mystical experience by taking a nap, but I did. I dropped out of ordinary time. I interrupted the algorithm of my everyday narrative and habits. My mental histrionics receded like low tide. Love entered the room. This light fed seeds of light deep within my soil, seeds I didn't know were there.

Who knew silence was a drug? Well, besides the Buddhists, the Trappists, and a few introverts. The quiet was thick. I felt grateful for every minute of it.

Then, right by my window, a lone songbird started singing. I wish I knew the type of bird. I am so bad with nature things. I wish I'd had an app. The bird sang so clearly, and *clearly to me*. It was like a tiny opera singer or Melissa Etheridge materializing on your balcony. Recital for the damaged. He was a Hindu priest chanting mantras. A cantor in synagogue. A messenger between the realms. Or maybe a high-end alarm clock from Bose. If I'd been in my head like usual, I don't even think I would have heard him.

Maybe that little visitor was attuning my vibration. Could the retreat center have trained this bird to sing to neurotics? Well then,

I'd definitely have to come here more often. I absorbed this invocation. Maybe the bird evangelist was calling evil spirits out of my body, along with regrets and failures and a ticker-tape parade of to-do lists. Maybe he was a dead relative, an ancestor returned to tell me that time is short and to get a better haircut. Or to get off my own damn back and cherish myself more.

That day I think I released my burdens, burdens that had been nested in other burdens. I couldn't have made this happen. It was just having the time and space to allow this process. Of course, it was more than just having taken a nap. It was the surrender of all my plans. It was allowing myself to feel good instead of doing the "good things" I should do for myself. That day I stopped trying. I didn't judge myself. I slipped into beingness. Yes, I still had hairy problems. But I'd tapped into my inner equilibrium. I was free.

I remember this experience so well because things began to shift in my life afterward. Out of the blue more help started showing up in my life. More clients. More flow. I think I'd stopped struggling. I surrendered. When I wasn't battling within as much, things started moving forward in my life. Don't ask me why. Don't ask me how. It's one of those woo-woo things that science will explain one day.

Meanwhile, I just know that taking space and being kind to myself is a bridge to other realms. I also know I resist it because part of me still thinks it's "smarter" to work hard, drag on, and not give in to weakness. I guess the "weakness" of one paradigm is the strength of another.

This is what I wrote in my journal that day. It was the voice of my inner teacher speaking and it said: *How you treat yourself is your prayer to me.*

I didn't realize or know that rest and sweetness were ways of praying. I didn't know that devotion to myself was devotion to my God.

I forgot that feeling barren wasn't just feeling normal. I forgot that all creative energy first requires a bath from the ordinary world. You can't just flip a switch or push your way through to deeper realms. Nurturing is a requirement. Self-care isn't optional. You don't get from frustrated, angry, and bitter to bliss, connection, and abundance. The realm of love requires love.

This is how you become present to a natural flow. You have to feel yourself, even the uncomfortable emotions. Befriend yourself. Stop resisting your inner climate and allow things to be as they are. That's when you can receive the message. *There will always be a shift awaiting you.* Healing wants to happen. Stop forcing and fighting and keeping the problems alive. Pause and rest. Love begets love. Love begets expansion.

SELF-TRUST INQUIRY

How can you take rest?
How do you take rest?
What gives you space between the worlds?

SELF-TRUST-ISMS

Rest Gives You Wings

If you want to be an eagle, you have to get off the hamster wheel.

When you do not rest, you hold yourself back from expansion.

....

A holy guided life requires space and time.

....

The more you wish to do in this life, the more you need to regenerate and recalibrate.

....

You can only perform according to the level of care you receive.

....

You may not hear your soul when your nervous system is bathed in cortisol. High alert is one frequency. Deep alert is another.

....

I forgot that feeling barren wasn't just feeling normal.

20

Get Honest. Get What You Want.

THE PRACTICE: Getting what you really want will flood you with energy and gratitude. You are here to respect your desires. Your inclinations are directives of your intuition. You may feel awkward about what you prefer. You may feel embarrassed or afraid to admit it. But it will drain you if you do not champion your needs. **Your practice is to pay attention to your intuition and ask for exactly what you want.** Dare to be honest, particular, and steadfast.

If Rosa Parks had taken a poll before she
sat down in the bus in Montgomery,
she'd still be standing.
—MARY FRANCES BERRY

Ask for what you want and be prepared to get it.
—MAYA ANGELOU

Self-care is soul care. It's giving your soul exactly what it wants and needs. It doesn't matter what your brain thinks you should need or should want. Soul care is not up for debate.

It's exhausting to deny your desires. It's debilitating to reject what you truly want and tell yourself you "shouldn't" need it. You crave what you crave because of an intelligent design.

A doctor doesn't prescribe stomach medicine for a heart problem and say, "Well, it's *close*. It's medicine. Stop being so nitpicky." No. You require precisely what you need to heal and thrive. Getting what you truly desire is prana, life-force energy. That's why I'll tell you to stop being so mealy-mouthed with yourself. Get honest. Get real. Get happy.

I know, I know. Sometimes you don't want to admit what you want. Let me share an example that may just change your mind.

"Oh, you don't want to go to *that* lake," said Martha, the blond Airbnb host, pushing her felt-covered homemade guidebook into my hands. "If you go to this one," she said, "it's pristine and you'll just love the drive there too." This was the "right lake." The air thickened and clotted with her suggestion.

I didn't want to go to that lake. My stomach tugged in resistance. I wanted to go back to Lake Taconic, the beach I knew. I wanted to swim along the ropes. Surrounded by families eating meatball subs and Cheetos. I wanted public bathrooms. I didn't want the Lonely Planet backpacking version of a lake.

Still, I hate being uncool. I wanted to please Martha, my Airbnb host, even though this was *my* vacation. Because naturally I needed this total stranger to be titillated by my choices. My EQ radar beeped and whistled as I watched her enthusiasm cool into brittle cordiality. Yikes, I was the boring Airbnb guest. She had pointed to the dark side of the moon, and I had chosen Hoboken, New Jersey.

The minute she left, self-doubt stung me like a swarm of country bees. I couldn't help but feel as though I was doing something wrong. Like maybe I was eating McDonald's in Paris. Like maybe I was *that* girl.

But I wasn't looking for novelty or adventure. I was looking for nurturing. I wanted a lake that was a *mensch,* a kindhearted natural body of water that posed no threat. I craved predictability because I'd had enough drama in real life.

I wanted nostalgia. I wanted to drink in the feelings of summer at the lake, just like times from my childhood. I didn't know this consciously. I was just moved and compelled to choose this lake.

I had been recovering from a hip injury. I didn't know how much I could swim. I didn't trust my body yet. I'd flown in from Denver partly to be back here. To swim in the kind of lake I fantasized about, the lakes from my childhood.

I didn't want to be somewhere unknown. I sure as hell didn't want to be somewhere *pristine*. Pristine sounded isolated and like there could be actual nature there, like ticks, swamp creatures, or bears. Not to mention rugged ax murderers.

Secretly I wanted to swim in a big bathtub steeped in memories. I love being surrounded by people. I love the accents and the intonations and absorbing the private, not-so-private conversations of others. It was as soothing as birdsong to me. It was birdsong. I am from New York City. People engage and calm me.

The next day, swimming along those bobbing ropes, I felt pure and holy and free. The feeling of comfort enabled me to relax.

I was so grateful to have gotten what I wanted, what I needed, what I craved. *Thank you, thank you, thank you*—that was the heartbeat I felt as I splashed in that great green body of water. I felt so happy I could have squealed like a baby pig. This was exactly what I wanted.

Children called "Marco Polo" to one another. A lifeguard blew a whistle occasionally for swimming infractions, or maybe just to remind us we were safe and supervised. I could feel the energy of all the families having a weekend, having time away from it all, stress melting under the blazing sun. I marinated in this peace.

It was mecca. The mecca my soul chose for this time. I knew I would heal my body in this water.

This satisfaction was like a massage that melts all pain away. Only this was a soul massage. I couldn't help but wonder how many other things would feel great in my life if I listened to myself more. I shuddered to think that I almost didn't come to this lake.

I had almost let my insane people pleaser run rampant and fawn over and please someone else, rejecting my needs. I had almost chosen to pose as "hip and interesting" instead of being real—honest with myself and with someone I would never even see again.

Turns you can't feel wholehearted joy if you're not being honest. Who knew?

Maybe as you read this, you'll **give yourself permission to do something "lame." Or strange, gung ho, or ridiculous by someone else's standards.** Listen to what you really want. Soul care is giving yourself what you crave.

YES, IT'S VULNERABLE ASKING FOR WHAT YOU REALLY WANT

Sometimes, it's hard to know what we want. Sometimes, it's hard to speak it. Yes, there are those plucky souls who actually ask for things easily. Maybe they stroll into the parent-teacher association meeting wearing thigh-high black leather boots with their list of demands. Like unicorns, they are as unself-conscious as the sun.

But many of us don't like to ask for things. We prefer to risk not doing what we want—rather than dare vulnerability. We pray that others figure out what we need, especially if we drop crafty, curated hints. Yet not using our God-given vocal cords just gets old.

Speaking of getting old, I have an example of the power of asking for what you need.

On a milestone birthday, I couldn't figure out how to celebrate. I knew a friend who had flown to Maui for a week of yoga and surfing for a significant birthday. And a client of mine bought himself a silver Mercedes-Benz sports car. But I didn't have their budgets or their inclinations. No, something in me hankered for something different.

Dare to be honest, particular, and steadfast.

I didn't want a chocolate cake. I didn't want a steak. I didn't want green eggs and ham. I wanted something unequivocally "Tam." I didn't want to get bombed in a club or anywhere. And most of all, I didn't want to let my indecision push me into making the day "no big deal" and glossing over the milestone. So I hunted inside myself for some communication.

I remembered reading in *The New Yorker* about an author who, when she got her first book published, chose to celebrate with flowers. Living in New York City, she went down to a local flower vendor on the street near where she lived. She purchased his entire stock of flowers, buckets of them. She filled her whole apartment with fresh-cut flowers, breathing in their scent for days.

I wanted to do something that honored me like this. Something outrageously significant. Something that felt like wrapping twinkle lights around my aging heart.

Finally, I settled on it. I would do a healing ritual. I would mark my time on earth burning some palo santo incense and white sage, instead of birthday candles. I created my own agenda for what I called a self-blessing ceremony.

I wanted to recount all the times I'd been brave, and all the times I was proud of. I would also thank myself for crawling through some years that felt as though I were an apartment building that had been gutted but not remodeled. Or other years that had me racing through a labyrinth as the *Jaws* soundtrack thundered in the background, while I told my family that everything was going great.

There was more to the ritual. I asked friends and loved ones to write me a note that I could open during the ceremony. I asked them to answer two specific questions. How do you see me? What do you wish for me? I even asked my older brother, though I imagined he saw my life as weird and on the flower-child spectrum. That felt scary. I reached out to a business colleague too, another risk.

Believe me, asking those questions of others felt embarrassing, as though I was fishing for love and compliments, and this, no less, was how I had decided to celebrate. If I thought about it much, it could make me feel as though I'd eaten bad sushi.

Who asks for direct feedback about themselves—for their birthday? I felt like some desperate lounge lizard reeking of Aqua Velva, chasing young women, making a spectacle of himself. The whole thing felt raw and obvious and could strike some judgmental types, like me, as needy.

Yet it also felt ballsy. Since I was getting older—and hell, making an event of it—I decided to stop wasting precious time. I asked for what I really wanted. I also made it a no-pressure request for the recipient. I was gracious in my email, and I had someone collect the email responses for me to create a buffer for everyone.

On the designated day, I started by doing an online Jivamukti yoga class. I knew that would zap me into a different state of energy right off the bat, assuming it didn't cripple or paralyze me first. Then I snacked on pistachio nuts, green grapes, and popcorn, the all-star lineup of favorite Tama snack foods. I would feast on takeout Thai food and Häagen-Dazs coffee ice cream after the ceremony.

Paul, my space-holding life partner, joined me in the ritual. I lit candles. I prayed. I spoke aloud. I cried. I spoke in stream of consciousness from my depths.

Memories arose as I invoked and honored them. I thanked each part of me I could think of at the time. I blessed the scenes in my life when things had been dicey or disappointing. I shouted like a gospel minister. I whispered like a librarian. I trembled, giggled, and cried. I have a feeling there was some snot involved.

I thanked myself for all the times I faced hard things, stupid hard things, and I kept showing up. Speaking these scenes aloud sparked spontaneous emotions, epiphanies, and more memories. It was a jumble and choreography of feelings and micro healings. By the time I finished speaking out loud, I was a grateful, hoarse, shining mess.

Then I opened my notes, one by one. I had saved their secret content for this final moment. I placed them on a table near an altar I had created. They winked like Christmas presents under a tree. I was already high on my own self-forgiveness and appreciation when I read them. Yet I squealed when I read the words from those who knew me. Each of them struck a sacred chord.

So many of the notes expressed similar observations. The repetition helped me trust the messages; the love overcame me. Through each email or handwritten note, I felt seen. Even and poignantly so from my brother. That day I got what I had always wanted from life. To be seen. To be loved. To be known. And to *feel* it.

It was a fiercely soul-satisfying birthday. An experience and education I'll take to my grave. I experienced this happiness not just because others said great things about me, but let's be real, people, that helped. No, I think the real joy was that I had heard myself at the deepest level. I allowed myself to go for it. I took the risk. I loved myself enough to ask for what I really wanted. And man, did I get it.

I hope you will love yourself enough in your lifetime to ask for what you really want.

SELF-TRUST INQUIRY

If you allowed yourself, what would you like to do?
If you allowed yourself, what would you like to ask for?

SELF-TRUST-ISMS

Get Honest. Get What You Want.

Self-care is soul care. It's giving your soul exactly what it wants and needs.

It doesn't matter what your brain thinks you should need or should want. Soul care is not up for debate.

It's exhausting to deny your desires.

Getting what you really want is prana, life-force energy.

··

Stop being so mealy-mouthed with yourself. Get honest.
Get real. Get happy.

··

Love yourself enough to ask for what you really want.

21

Think Twice Before You're Nice

THE PRACTICE: Your soul care requires you to trust what you need. You have a right to your own rhythms, desires, and inclinations. Boundaries are a form of mindfulness. Your mindful boundaries can never threaten a real relationship. You have a responsibility to do your soul's work. **Your practice is to become intentional about your time and energy.**

Daring to set boundaries is about having the courage to love ourselves, even when we risk disappointing others.
—BRENÉ BROWN

If you do not respect your own wishes, no one else will.
—VIRONIKA TUGALEVA

"I never find time for me," says Maureen. "I always think I'll have time to meditate or take out a paintbrush and paint, but I don't know where the hours go." Maureen tells me more about her life. It's obvious where the hours go. She has a demanding mother, husband, boss, dog, and position on the board of a dysfunctional nonprofit. Maureen makes sure everyone else gets what they need. The woman is a saint. The woman is angry.

I begin my sales pitch. "What if you didn't see painting as just fun? What if you saw it as medicine, a pharmaceutical-grade serotonin uptake? Or a devotion to God like transcribing a holy scripture?" I ask. "Or what if meditation is the way you 'put your oxygen mask on first' so that you can continue to help those you love?"

Maureen has a story that her desires are frivolous, and I'm telling her the story of why they will save her life. **Our lives depend on our priorities. Because one thing I know for sure. We will never find time. We will take it.**

I'll bet you a Starbucks coffee that Martin Luther King Jr. said no to playing mah-jongg—or perhaps even to a meeting about saving baby seals since that wasn't the cause that beat the bongos in his heart. He said yes to his assignment—the one life that called to him. He wasn't selfish. *He was intentional.* It takes intentionality to create a life that reverberates with love, authenticity, and impact.

Can you say "boundaries"? I've never liked the word. I imagine barbed wire or a mean woman with blunt bangs. But boundaries are a form of mindfulness. **It's not about rejecting someone else. It's about refusing to reject your own desires and needs.** Where do you leak strength or focus? Losing time is like losing blood. *Because time and attention create your dreams.*

YOU HAVE A RESPONSIBILITY TO YOURSELF

You have sacred work to do—and it may even be the work of grieving or healing a situation in your life. This is your one life. It's time to start realizing that your needs matter. You have a right to your rhythm and your inclinations.

Still, the people in your life may fling casual social norms or expectations your way, like tossing horseshoes at a backyard barbecue. Step away from the barbecue. Think like a maverick or a monk. Pay attention to the light or inner necessity that calls to you right now. Be intentional.

I know you may want to be liked or fit in. You don't want to create waves, piss off Uncle Bob, or deal with your sister who thinks you are being selfish and inhumane because you refuse to go with her to get a pedicure. Authenticity takes courage. Clarissa Pinkola Estés, author of *Women Who Run with the Wolves,* says, "To be ourselves causes us to be exiled by many others, and yet to comply with what others want causes us to be exiled from ourselves."

We will never find time. We will take it.

I used to have a hard time saying no to lunch dates. "You have to eat," someone would say. I'd think I "should" go. Then I'd eat my heart out when I'd eat with them. I wanted time to write my book, or to putter in preparation of writing. I ached when I did not write. I ached when I abandoned myself. Every time I said yes to a meeting I didn't really want to do, I'd said no to my dream. The second I casually said, "Oh, sure, what time works for you?" I could have smacked myself.

Others thought, what's the big deal? You're just spending an hour eating a Cobb salad—how bad could that be? But then there was traffic, road closures, a tiny little five-hour stop to pick up something along the way, a slow waitstaff, possible alien invasions, and *small talk*. Then the backlash of self-recrimination, the desire to scrub myself of every mewling accommodating cell of my body. It was obvious that I'd require an exorcism to evict the demon of She Who Will Not Cause Conflict and Swallows Her Own Bile.

Next came the phone calls to friends to hyperventilate and vent, and, naturally, the Netflix binge and vat of ice cream to soothe my nerves now that the day was an official wreck. Nothing in this lifetime is just an hour. Especially nothing that is wrong for us.

TAKING CARE OF YOURSELF SERVES OTHERS (IN WAYS YOU CAN'T IMAGINE!)

My life partner, Paul, is a Georgia peach of a human being and a giver in every cell of his being. In recent years, however, he's suffered from a complicated fatigue condition. It's forced him to respect his limits and say no, even if he feels like he's letting someone else down. Even if that someone else is as adorable as me.

One Saturday we came home from one of my speaking engagements. I was flying high; Paul felt beat. We'd planned to go car shopping together when we got home—because he was Mr. Consumer Reports and knew things about cars and I didn't. He bowed out to take a nap instead. So much for car shopping.

At first, I felt disappointed, though with an evolved flair, of course. I was proud of Paul for taking care of himself. Still I felt like the kid in summer who doesn't know what to do with herself. After my events I tend to have crazy high energy—and can't just sit and read or chill.

Ooh, I could go look at furniture in that Asian décor store on Broadway. The thought wafted in like the scent of lilacs. I'd wanted to check the place out forever, but I never had time. Just like that, I was off on my own adventure.

The place was huge, bigger than I had imagined. Jackpot! They were having a wild one-day sale. I couldn't believe the markdowns. I found an antique Chinese red wedding cabinet for my office for an absurdly low price. I thought I'd died and gone to chic bargain heaven. I walked around a little more and just as I was about to leave, I found another room.

Stashed in the corner, I discovered these creative Buddha paintings by a Thai artist. For years, I'd been looking for something special for my living room. I found not one, but two paintings I loved. These pieces were higher priced, but because of the sale, I could make the stretch. I was drooling. I imagined my sweet Paul drooling on our couch taking his nap. Maybe we were connected in the dream time.

This sparkling stream of interconnected events continued. "Oh, you're buying *both* those paintings?" said the happy shopkeeper. "That artist is a new vendor for us. I wasn't sure if I'd bring in any other paintings from him. Now we will."

I imagined a thin young man in a remote Thai village getting a call that his art had just sold in America. I imagined him telling his wife and her hurrying to the marketplace. Later they would sit down to a specially prepared fish dinner, hopefully giggling. I imagined him painting the next morning, knowing his work was wanted—and wanted in an international market. Wow, how lucky we all were that Paul had taken a nap.

It seems to me that when we listen to our own authentic truth, we are valuing an intelligent instruction. We are part of some intricate constellation of grace that advances everyone. For all I know, maybe the fish vendor who sold the fish to my imaginary Thai wife had a miracle too. I like to think the chain of good is still going on.

YOU CAN'T RUFFLE REAL LOVE
(AND YOU DON'T WANT ANYTHING ELSE)

Often, we're afraid to honor our boundaries because we don't want to ruffle others—or risk losing connection. When we first start taking care of ourselves, there can be pushback. Some people will balk and suggest that you're being weird, a bummer, or joining a cult. They'll actually say that *you* are being selfish—because you're not doing what *they* want. You never used to be this way.

But before you cave in to obedience, penance, and promising away your weekends for the next millennium, remember this: **Real relationships support the real you. You can never lose authentic love by being who you really are.**

Then there are the energy vampires, those individuals sent straight from heaven and put on planet Earth to force you to grow a pair. These caring souls will stop at nothing until you have nothing—or until you say "uncle" and draw a boundary.

I remember driving to Northern California getting ready to lead a retreat. Stopping for a break, I wandered into a small boutique with painted scarves in its windows. It looked like my kind of store, and I was looking forward to maybe finding something special to take with me to the retreat.

The minute I entered the store, the owner, a tiny woman with tight black curls, scooted over to me and started talking like a wind-up doll. She told me about the sales. I smiled. Then she told me about the rugs she had just imported from Turkey . . . and then about her flight to Turkey . . . and how her flights usually go . . .

I kept trying to focus on the rack of exotic scarves. The wind-up doll continued talking but I no longer found her socially appropriate. I was beginning to want to howl, or at the very least, scream at the top of my lungs—"Leave me alone!" But I didn't want to be rude. Besides, I teach *A Course in Miracles* which is all about seeing the light in others, though this woman was seriously draining my generator. I also have Golden Retriever in my DNA. A floppy, sloppy need to be kind and to love everyone! Not to mention, to get praise and treats!

But I felt irritated, because my "fun little break" was evaporating. I was tired of nodding and forcing smiles. I imagined pinning her against the wall and shrieking, "Leave me alone, woman— have you no mercy or decency at all?" Finally, I said aloud, "I'm just going to look around on my own." This is as direct as I get, people. I even deliberately walked to the other side of the shop. But get this. *She followed me.* She continued telling her next story without a pause. She spoke *louder.* I was trapped in this blabber vortex.

That's when it hit me. *She didn't care at all about what I wanted. I didn't need to be nice to someone who had no respect for me.* I didn't say a word. I walked out of the shop, letting the little bells on the door tinkle as I left. I breathed in the salt air of that small ocean town and skipped back to my rental car. I was a ladybug who had just escaped a spider's web. I was a freaking bald eagle.

I will always advocate being kind to others in this world. Yet think twice before you're "nice." Nice can be a sugar-coated pill of self-rejection. Your desires matter, and doing what matters should never be sacrificed for a false idea of manners.

Besides, real kindness feels great.

SELF-TRUST INQUIRY

Where do you need to draw a boundary in your life?
Where do you tend to people-please or be "nice"
at the cost of your own desires?

SELF-TRUST-ISMS

Think Twice Before You're Nice

Boundaries are a form of mindfulness. It's not about rejecting someone else. It's about refusing to reject your own.

Our lives depend on our priorities ... We will never find time. We will take it.

It was obvious that I would require an exorcism to evict the demon of She Who Will Not Cause Conflict and Swallows Her Own Bile.

Nothing in this lifetime is just an hour. Especially nothing that is wrong for us.

Real relationships support the real you. You can never lose authentic love by being who you really are.

Think twice before you're "nice." Nice can be a sugar-coated pill of self-rejection.

KICKSTARTS AND PRACTICES

Have at it. Play with these. Trust yourself. Go where you're guided . . .

Pick Three Self-Trust-isms from Part V. Journal about them. Maybe do make some art. Meditate or reflect on the words that spoke to you. Discuss them with someone else. Let these chosen phrases unlock a new awareness and conversation within.

1. **Become a Compassionate Witness.** What part of you needs love right now? Write about this part of yourself in the third person. For example, *[your name here]* is doing so well and is going through *[fill in the blank]* and needs *[fill in the blank]*. Elaborate!
2. **The Care and Feeding of You.** What feeds you most? Spiritual community? Nature? Running? Reggae? Create a customized resource list you continue to develop. What can you do for five minutes a day? Once a week? Once a month? What draining activity can you *not* do?
3. **Personal Bill of Rights.** Create a list of your self-care rights, affirming the responsibility you have for your own well-being. Include rest, boundaries, and fun.
4. **Sanctuary Day.** Give yourself a day or part of one to *just be*. Rest on a hammock, pray, or go for a meditative walk. Listen to music or paint. Resist the urge

to be "productive." Allow yourself to feel lonely or unmoored. Open to surprise.

5. **Soul-Care Collage.** Create a collage of images, quotes, and activities that feel rejuvenating to you. Display your collage to remind you of how you want to feel— and to help you prioritize self-care.

6. **You Deserve a Celebration.** Create your own ritual or adventure to mark something meaningful to you. This could be very small, elaborate, or ongoing. Would you like to involve others?

PART VI

From Helplessness to Self-Empowerment

OWNING YOUR INTREPID SPIRIT

THE BLOCK: Helplessness
THE BREAKTHROUGH: *Self-Empowerment*

YOU GET IN YOUR OWN WAY
when you believe you are helpless or incompetent.

YOU DISCOVER YOUR OWN WAY
when you practice feeling empowered.

You may not trust yourself because you believe you are helpless. Incompetent. A freak show. Trampled grass. Fill in the blank.

But what if only a part of you feels helpless? What if another part of you knows it can accomplish anything? Like right now. Like yesterday.

You trust and empower yourself when you side with your own blazing potential. You have bold, transcendent powers—and it's time to stop forgetting who you are.

Here's what siding with your potential looks like. Now you refuse to listen to any voice that negates your promise. You take actions with patience, focus, and encouragement. You stop resisting what is. You believe in your path and seize the opportunities in front of you.

I invite you to leap into the life that will make you believe in who you always knew you could be.

In this section we will work with how to activate and stay connected to your light. With that kind of love, there's very little you can't do.

22

Entering the Crucible

THE PRACTICE: You may lack confidence, but you do not lack power. You may be afraid to try new things, to do it "wrong." But with patience and compassion, you can learn how to do anything you need to do. Empowerment is the choice to love yourself enough to face new challenges—and awaken a new identity. **Your practice is to remind yourself that you can do anything you need to do.**

When I let go of what I am,
I become what I might be.
—LAO TZU

Life begins at the end of your comfort zone.
—NEALE DONALD WALSCH

Some of you may feel like you can do anything. You can bush-whack your way through an off-grid jungle or read instructions for yourself and install things. You may even love pitting your smarts against the brute encounter of the unknown. Not me. I am not confident when I am facing new things. In fact, I am doing spectacularly if I'm not having an anxiety attack.

When I first became a writer, as in one who would write and then seek publication, I felt puny and vulnerable. Then later, as a creative turned entrepreneur and business owner, I felt lost at sea without oars in my rowboat. Throughout my life, I have imagined I was powerless and incompetent.

Typically, I assume, no, *I know,* that everyone else knows how to do everything with synchronized perfection—like the Rockettes or Swiss watchmakers with tiny spectacles—and honestly this makes me want to give up my dreams and go home.

However, I am moving past helplessness and it's like seeing the sun rise for the first time.

I want to take you with me. If you have ever felt inept as though you can't run a business or your family's schedule, write a song, find a lover or an answer, or roll up your yoga mat evenly, which, personally I think is a covert form of hell invented by kindergarten teachers, I want to tell you a story about going past imaginary limits. It's a story of self-forgiveness. It's a story of actualizing your full potential. Actually, it's a story of folding a goddamn blanket. But it's really a story of *unfoldment,* of how you can teach yourself to do anything in this world you want or need to do.

I'd been visiting a friend who is a famous author and speaker and staying in her charming guesthouse in San Francisco. "What do you want me to do with the bedding?" I ask her that night because I'm leaving early the next morning and won't see her. "Oh, fold the blanket back up and leave it at the foot of the bed with the others," she says casually. I try not to twitch or gulp. I feel the elevator going down in my stomach.

Oh crap, I think. It's as though she had said, "Oh, just be a normal person"—which in my case is the equivalent of saying, "Take a flying leap at the moon." They are one and the same. I was hoping she would say, "Just leave it in a reckless heap like you leave everything. I'll take care of it. I'll be the good mommy. I am an adult and I know how to do things." No such luck. I am on my own here. With bedding issues. In front of someone I admire and secretly want to impress. I desperately do not want to expose my deplorable inner limitations.

In the morning, I get dressed and pack up my jumbled suitcase. I'm ready to leave and the only thing I need to do is face the dreaded task of folding the blanket. I stare at the crumpled outrage. Obviously, I was fighting Godzilla in my sleep. Then I study the other white blankets at the foot of the bed, deriding me, white cotton folded with German engineering, resting like smug doves. The bar is high.

My stomach clenches. I am going to screw this up. *I am a screw-up.* I am going to create a lumpy, ugly, bulging, inept pile that announces either raw disregard or reprehensible incompetence. I consider writing a note apologizing. I feel like an idiot. Folding things neatly—I missed that class in first grade. I was probably having a cigarette or a Jujube.

I am totally intimidated by this inanimate white bed cover. But, really, it's the shame of being me. How are you a woman of a certain age and you do not know how to fold a blanket neatly? *I never had a mother teach me*, a little one whispers within. Later, I realize, I bet my mother never had a mother teach her either. But at the time, I was only angry at *my* mother for not providing the skills, the fundamentals of being a functioning adult woman in this world. Then, of course, I haven't been willing to learn these basics either. I prefer to skate by. This, too, fills me with self-recrimination.

I'm going to do this wrong. I'm going to make a mess. These fears stop me from trying anything new in my life. *You can do this*, I tell myself. *Be patient*, whispers a quiet voice of grandeur within. *Look at it. Decide that you can.* With this mercy, I begin to break out of the tractor beam of learned helplessness. It doesn't matter if I have felt incompetent for a thousand years.

You can do anything you need to do.

Helplessness is an electric fence around me, but it turns out that I can turn off the current at any time. It's not just here in my example of folding the blanket. It's everywhere in my life. I've been learning to question the part of me that says, *I can't do it. I will never be able to do this. I won't do it right or like other well-adjusted, well-cared-for people would do it.*

For example, I had just been telling my friend that night that I am going beyond learned helplessness in my business. I have been terrified of hiring people, of doing it wrong, making a grim mistake, spending gobs of money, *wasting* money. In the past, I wanted to get it over with, be at some finish line, *phew,* and completely duck out of that nerve-racking thing called process. I didn't trust myself. I didn't trust that I could learn what I needed or discover my own system for finding good hires.

In fact, years ago, I paid a company to hire for me. It was a disaster which led to even more self-doubt. Yet in hindsight, I get it. The wisdom of the Universe wouldn't allow me to play "pass the hot potato" with my issues or skip the opportunity to step into my own empowerment and confidence. Oh, how *thoughtful* is this Universe.

This is what I have learned:

Empowerment is a choice.

It's a choice to go slow.

It's a choice to be present.

Empowerment is a choice to love yourself while you face any challenge that holds you back from full expression.

This time, as I begin to hire different positions in my business,

I am ready to take my sweet time. I am ready and willing to make mistakes. I am ready to experiment, stumble, fall, and keep going. I am not going to allow frustration to have the final say. I will be unstoppable. It's self-love that gives me these muscles.

Now about that blanket. *Make this go away, make this go away,* my impatience and desperation, twin gargoyles, howl in fierce unison. Instead, I turn and face the blanket. I will not allow my fears to turn into facts any longer. It's only my belief that I can't do something that has kept me from doing it. Now, I have created a new teacher-mother-authority-empress within me. She whispers: *We can do this, honey. We'll just take as long as we need. We'll learn as we go.*

I decide to stop assuming I can't do things. I am going to start assuming that I can—and not only that, but with the requisite time and self-love, I can crush it.

Let me tell you what else happened the day I folded the blanket. I didn't just forgive myself. I forgave my mother. I walked beyond my history. First, I stood before that blanket as though I was naked, on trial, and on camera. Like maybe my friend had surveillance cameras on. Like maybe the whole world has surveillance on. Yes, because my every mundane move is just so important.

Then, at last, I slow down and face the task before me, even as everything within me wants to bolt, end the friendship, call her names, and take up residence off the grid though near a coffee shop. Instead, I listen to thoughts that set me free: *I don't have to allow this blanket to make me feel bad about myself. There is no shame in feeling that something is a challenge. I am not broken. I am inexperienced. I am not powerless.*

That's when I flash on memories of my mother. She wasn't a very good housekeeper. Often my father would yell at her, call her ugly names, and as he did with all of us, he would grab any task away from her. My mother also didn't have any interest in learning how to improve, even years later when she was free of my father.

I am my mother's daughter. I haven't wanted to learn either. I mean, there's Google, for God's sake, where I could probably learn how to *competitively* fold a blanket. But I don't care. I just want to be rescued. Could I call TaskRabbit and have an anal high school student come to fold this blanket? I kid you not. The thought crossed my mind.

Finally, that morning, I decide to fold the blanket with Zen attention, devotion, and care, because I am sick to my spleen of feeling incompetent and living in secret. I am going to rescue myself. I am going to face the summit, the monster, the shame. *I am going to walk beyond, Mommy,* I say to myself. *I am going to go where you have never been. I am going to take your shame, my shame, and who knows if there are generations of this self-punishment, and I am going to stop it.*

This is my new truth. I am going to clean up this pain. Even though shame sometimes feels like a gray sop bucket overflowing. Even if it seems impossible. I am going to start small and do what I can. *I am not going to be your daughter anymore in that way, Mommy.* I am not going to blame you. I am not going to tell the story to others or myself, the one that says it's because you never taught me.

I will teach myself. I will learn. I will heal. I will fold a goddamn blanket and be a goddess in this world. I will write books, hire teams, and I will lead leaders. I will stand on top of a mountain you couldn't climb, and I won't do it out of anger or to make you wrong. I will do it for both of us. I will do it and transform the places where we were abandoned or abandoned ourselves.

We are good enough. We are capable. We are worthy. We can do this.

I can do this.

I will do this.

I folded that blanket. It looked shockingly normal. *I made us look normal, Mommy,* I whispered within. When I left that place I left with more than a folded blanket behind.

Turns out, you can do anything you decide to do.

SELF-TRUST INQUIRY

What is your blanket? Where are you assuming
that you can't do something?
Would you be willing to face this challenge with all the
time you need . . . and the belief that you can do it?

SELF-TRUST-ISMS

Entering the Crucible

....

You may lack confidence, but you do not lack power.

....

You can do anything you need to do.

....

Empowerment is a choice to love yourself while you face
any challenge that holds you back from full expression.

....

It's only my belief that I can't do something that has kept
me from doing it.

....

....

I decide to stop assuming I can't do things. I am going to start assuming that I can.

....

There is no shame in feeling that something is a challenge. I am not broken. I am inexperienced. I am not powerless.

23

There's Something You Can Do Right Now

THE PRACTICE: We get in the way of our own progress, telling ourselves what we can't do. Or what we should have done. If you want to move forward in something you desire, **your practice is to ask yourself: What can I do right now?** There is always something you can do right now. Empowerment comes from being present and approaching the situation with new eyes and a willing heart.

Do what you can, with what you have, where you are.
—THEODORE ROOSEVELT

Inaction breeds fear and doubt.
—DALE CARNEGIE

I am, as usual, gritting my way through this level 2/3 yoga class, which is packed because Denver is nothing if not crammed with mountain bikers, skiers, climbers, and early-morning fitness freaks. I'm sitting there on my mat listening to chant music and softly feeling crappy, because I am telling myself hideous things about myself and my life.

I should be further along. I am self-employed and I don't know where my good is coming from in the next few months. I want guarantees. I want results. *Other people get to have solid lives and jet off to Madrid or buy anything they want at Whole Foods,* I think. Everyone else is a grown-up who has it all mapped out for life.

Of course, I'm delusional—but you rarely know that when you're self-absorbed. That Saturday there should be a little picture of me next to the word "self-absorbed" in *Webster's Dictionary.* Or maybe I am just hurting like a pulsing tooth.

Then I see him, a man in his mid-thirties, and he has two poles, like ski poles. Maybe they are ski poles. Or canes. He is doing yoga.

As I look over at him, I realize that both of his legs are deformed, twisted and smaller. They are like saplings, the trunks of very young trees, and they seem bent in the wind, collapsing in on each other even as they stand. There he is, moving into Warrior Two pose. I am instantly humbled and throbbing with inspiration. I burst with pride for this mangled stranger.

Here's what moves me. He is doing what he can do. He is not giving up. He is not bemoaning what is. He is not wearing a T-shirt that says, "Look at me and look at what happened to me, you idiot!" He is doing what he can do at this moment, which is really what life and yoga are all about. He is doing the best of what he can do, and he is doing *more* than what most people do.

I am more enthralled by him than by any influencer or celebrity on Instagram, even if they have a very cute Chihuahua or a bazillion followers. As class goes on, I am trying not to stare, though I have now decided he is my own personal TED Talk.

He is sharing every principle you've ever heard in a motivational speaker's speech, but he isn't saying a word.

Obviously, I have the insane good fortune to have my yoga mat positioned next to this Olympic champion as he brings home the gold. But this guy isn't bringing home the gold. He's bringing home the scrap metal. He's not in a championship. He is just going up against the ravages of life. *He is showing up.*

Sure, maybe I am idealizing this dude. Maybe he is in a bad mood, plotting revenge or composing hate mail in his head. Or he's just thinking about chowing down a burger after class. Whatever is going on for him that Saturday, he is my miracle.

I used to hear the term "self-mastery" and imagine people who walked on hot coals or who swallowed fire. This always seemed a bit theatric to me. If you ask me, life is hard enough without combustion. But really, **self-mastery may just be the art of going past your ego, your negative inner self-talk, and doing what you can do.**

Surprise, surprise, but doing what you can do turns out to be more than you would think.

Doing what you can do gives you a new vista and shows you possibilities you didn't know existed. Right action is a passport into another world.

It's never too late to do what you can do. I remember a time when I had just finished leading an amazing extended retreat at the Kripalu Center in the Berkshires. The glow was palpable. Yet as participants hugged goodbye and left, I felt this hot flash of anger toward myself.

Yes, I felt great about having created a space of love and breakthroughs for everyone. Still, I was beating myself up because I had casually betrayed myself. I hadn't asked for video testimonials. A business advisor had told me to do this during the retreat, but I felt too uncomfortable. Now I had let this perfect opportunity pass me by.

The bad voice within had a field day: *This is so you. You don't do anything to market yourself. Other presenters are recording videos with drones and fireworks, and you didn't even ask one single person for a testimonial.*

I was talking to Caryn, one of the retreatants, afterward and finally confided in her about my testimonial debacle. I am nothing if not authentic. "Why not do a Zoom call later this week with different students and film them then?" she asked. "No, that won't work," I said, sharing my reasons, good ones all. She offered another possibility, but I shook my head in negation. Her ideas didn't work for me. It was just too late. I'd messed up.

Finally, Caryn shot back, "Well, you keep telling me what you can't do. What *can* you do?" This question stepped forward as a shimmering blue-black African queen who parted the garbage pile of my restricting assumptions. The question was a pattern interrupt, like throwing a fish in my face.

What can you do right now?
Not . . . what haven't you done?

I was set on autopilot. I was doomed. I was in a familiar, though semi-unconscious, pattern of impotency. Caryn was all fired up from *my* retreat. This was rather inconvenient for the part of me that was happy to stay stuck. Caryn wouldn't back down.

"What can you do?" Her question ignored the past. She flung open the door to the holy present. Who was she, the Dalai Lama now? But she invited me into wonder territory, an exploration beyond my conditioned thought.

"Well, I could record a testimonial from you," I said. It fell out of my mouth. I practically choked on saying it. I felt self-conscious as well as horribly self-serving. But I said it, albeit froggy voiced, and like a little girl. I said what I could do now. That's when the party started.

"Let's do it," she said without a second of hesitation. She brushed her hair and I fumbled with my iPhone camera in disbelief. Caryn found and stood in front of a decorative room divider. "This is what I loved about the retreat," she began. We filmed my first video testimonial. Raw. Right then and there, two minutes after I said what I could do.

Then another student came back into the room, and Caryn and I asked permission to record him. We found two other students in the dining room who immediately said yes to saying something on video for just a minute. It was fast and simple. It was even fun, for all of us. I didn't know if I would use any of it, but it was what I could do. It was *something*. Let me tell you, I was wildly redeemed by doing it.

Your spiritual genius is always present, and always operates in the here and now. What can you do right now? Not what have you done or what haven't you done? Not why haven't you done it? But what can you do . . . now?

This kind of self-redemption drives up in a Maserati. It's racy. Self-love isn't mewling. Self-love takes you to the mat and empowers you to show up wherever you are—with what you've got. As it turns out, it's always enough. It gets the party started.

SELF-TRUST INQUIRY

Where have you felt like you can't do something?
Or that you didn't do something you should have?
What simple thing can you do right now?

SELF-TRUST-ISMS

There's Something You Can Do Right Now

Self-mastery may just be the art of going past your ego, your negative inner self-talk, and doing what you can do.

Doing what you can do gives you a new vista . . . Right action is a passport into another world.

It's never too late to do what you can do.

It was what I could do. It was *something*. Let me tell you, I was wildly redeemed by doing it.

What can you do right now? Not . . . what haven't you done?

Self-love isn't mewling. Self-love takes you to the mat and empowers you to show up wherever you are—with what you've got.

24

Instructions for Your Brave Place

THE PRACTICE: The path of empowerment begins when you feel defeated. This is the moment when you can make the most progress. Your habitual blocks will surface. Now you have the chance to leave them behind. **Your practice is to stop resisting the difficulty.** Show up. Slow down. Be compassionate with yourself. Let go of timing. Be willing to know you have a way to move through. This is where things are going to get *really* good.

This is what I tell my writing students: disappointment is where the journey begins. Because now you have a choice. How will you respond? Will you give up? Or will you show up—be with your situation and not duck out?
—TAMA KIEVES, from one of my courses

When we least expect it, life sets us a challenge to test our courage and willingness to change.
—PAULO COELHO

Nobody likes to feel stuck. It feels so powerless and, well, *stuck*. I'm sick of telling myself lies. I'm sick of playing small. I'm going to channel some inner Joan of Arc instead of Chicken Little. I know I'm blessed. I know we all have radical abilities. I know that every bump in the road is a bump up if we use it.

When you feel defeated, this is where things are about to get *really fluid*. This is where the path of self-trust can make all the difference. Your own mindfulness can take you to *a whole new level of progress*.

Disappointment or uncertainty can trigger the old machinery within us. Familiar thoughts crush us. Your stomach might feel heavy, a sack of wet sand. Or your heart beats as though you are a rabbit in headlights, and not a grown-up who has faced a trillion difficult things before.

I don't know about you, but the bully within beats me with repetition. *You are broken and you have always been small and weak.* I feel myself falling, falling, falling down the well. *You will always be inferior. You will always be stuck.* This sick advisor has me believing in a life of permanent helplessness. Yet I am learning how to see my painful emotions as opportunities to grow into a new identity.

This means I practice holding two things at once: the pain of where I am, and the faith of where I am. I let myself feel the pain. At the same time, I hold a perspective of *willingness* to believe in my path. For example, **I don't have to believe there is a brilliant transformation at work. I just have to be willing to believe.** It's the Jedi pivot that changes everything.

Here's my **Code of Willingness.** Take it for a spin:

I am willing to stop resisting this moment: I'm going to stop telling myself, I don't want to be here.

I am willing to believe that something will shift in a better direction—when it's the right time.

I am willing to know that deep love or truth always prevails, no matter the appearances.

I am willing to continue showing up. I am willing to give myself another chance.

I am willing to go into the black woods of any situation with one small flickering candle.

I am willing—because I want to know how far self-trust will take me.

I will not abandon myself. I will give my truth time and attention. I will endure because I am worth endurance. I will work with sacred powers even when I feel I have no power. I will walk right through a brick wall—and discover that I had been making my fears solid instead of myself.

Maybe you just can't figure out how to move on from a tortured relationship, get a paying client, or lose those thirty pounds. Pick your monkey, it doesn't matter, because every problem is your guru, your sensei, the customized badass that is going to take you further into your own indispensable capacities. It sounds glorious. It *is* glorious. But first it sucks. It gets your attention.

The practice of an inspired life is one of transcending limitations. Unfortunately—and I'm just not fond of this part at all—we encounter limitations. We signed up here for growth school, not coast school. Our "issues" are starting points. They're the buds and embryos of progress.

The philosopher Friedrich Nietzsche reminds us that on this ultimate adventure, we are *always* making progress. He says, "In the mountains of truth, you never climb in vain. Either you already reach a higher point today, or you exercise your strength in order to be able to climb higher tomorrow." This makes sense. Still, defeatism is a beast.

If you're facing your mountain, I have another mini creed for you. I wrote it when I was facing discouragement and it helped me approach my blocks differently.

FACING YOUR BLOCK CREED

I am going to stop wishing this situation away.
　　I am going to face the "block" with all the self-compassion I can muster. I have been building up to this moment. I have what it takes to expand and experience new power.

Breathe. This is not a problem. This is a soul adventure.
　　This is where things are going to get large.

I have gone as far as I know how to go. And I'm still not giving up. Breathe. I am taking my next step. This is new territory—and it will bring new results.

Just so you know, when I'm facing my own pain, I'm not Ms. Positive or Deepak Chopra or one of the church ladies who jump up in tears saying, "Praise, praise, praise!" I don't think things are anywhere near as terrific as tiramisu or getting my way. No, I'm just tired. I'm sick of feeling desperate, powerless, and a tiny bit furious. I need to move forward. I am willing. *I will not fail myself.*

I don't really know how to move forward. But that's the point. The smaller me is sucking her thumb while giving life the finger. The bigger me is opening to the invisible love and power in this situation, that which is beyond my old ways of seeing myself. I am not *giving up*—but I am *giving in* to this wretched, beautiful process. I know this is where I will meet my God or the strength that will cocreate with me. I know I will even look back some day and appreciate just how much I grew. I am so not there yet, and that's okay. This is my brave place.

> *I will endure because*
> *I am worth endurance.*

For me, life opens up when I finally decide not to indulge the rant of my resistance. *I don't want it to be this way. I just want to get what I want. I just want this to go away.* It's the cries of a two-year-old within me. She is terrified, loud, and entitled.

Freedom comes when I stop thinking this reactive inner voice represents *my* truth. She is a part of me. She is not, however, the part of me that welcomes expansion. I need to cradle her with kindness. "There, there, little one. I hear you. It's okay." I acknowledge the grief, fear, or ridiculous urge to break someone else's toy.

It's okay to feel bad. It's understandable to feel anxious when the amygdala part of my brain is screaming, "Annihilation is imminent. Clear the decks. Your email did not get a response. I repeat, annihilation is imminent." I can honor my "big feelings," as a friend of mine likes to say. But I will not make decisions about my future or operate heavy machinery while under their influence.

When I'm ready, I am willing to give my situation to my Big Mind or Higher Self. I am willing to believe in a bus driver or a loving reality that has a broader perspective and a few tricks up its sleeve. I am willing to consider that I am more than my disquieted mind or diminished self. My pain is a perspective or a flood of hormones coursing through me; pain is not my identity or destiny. I will not choose from my self-attack or sabotage. **Empowerment is making our decisions from our strength instead of our pain.**

This is spiritual surrender, and it is magic. It's a process of letting go of *your idea of what is going on,* so that you can finally hear your deeper intelligence or open to something new. Don't be surprised if things lift in ways that feel as though someone has pulled some strings for you behind the curtain. You have woken up in an entirely different movie. But first, you have to get sick of fighting what is. You have to release that death grip you have on your plans. Truth requires that we become available to *what is.*

Surrender isn't resignation. You can stay true to your desires, but perhaps not your timing or how it translates into form. Make room for genius or possibilities you can't see. Become humble, not crippled. In psychological and spiritual circles, I think they call this getting the hell out of your own way. Maybe this is the special path for control freaks like me. Maybe you're a control freak too, learning to trust the awe and consistency of a higher love.

SURRENDER, CREATIVITY, AND GROWTH

In some areas of my life, I really do know how to let go of control in favor of surprise leaps. Writing is like this for me. When I work on a project, things can be cloudy, brutal, and unbudging. I bring in patience, focus, and commitment. And nothing can withstand my commitment.

I am willing to surrender my doubts, my sense of timing, and my resistance. No matter what comes up, I will sort it out. This is my self-love and self-trust in action. I continuously show up with willingness or something like it. I keep writing my dull sentences. I keep untangling knots. I deliberately slow myself down. Then a thousand blue birds appear out of nowhere and I can't write fast enough to capture the love that is moving through me. Now I am dripping in sweat and gratitude for the work my smaller self could not have done alone—and for the process of trusting this unseen grace to knit my life together.

As I hit a block in other areas of my life, I tell myself the inspired process is the same. I will accept this juncture of my life just as it is—or at least die trying. I will lay down self-pity, yet deepen self-compassion for the part of me that is facing the wilderness or climbing her mountain. This is my moment. This is my portal. This is my process of going beyond my stuck places into new heights.

When you're frustrated, remember this can be your brave place. The juice is in this experience, not some moment in the future. *There is something here for you.* Can you stop fighting this life of yours? Can you start listening to this life of yours? Become curious. Suspend gloom or fury the second you can.

I'm a student of yoga and I know that with practice and focus the impossible becomes possible. My tendons ease with breath and stretching. Nothing is permanently stuck.

This is true in life too. No moment ever stays the same. My body is elastic. My mind is elastic. My future is elastic. Even my past is elastic because I can change how I understand or interpret it.

If you're feeling stuck at all, here's my recipe. Sit down. Breathe. Open your heart to yourself. **Mark this holy time in your mind. This is the border between where you've been and everything you want.** Stretch or move forward with presence. You are moving past the old regime of negative thinking that you may have always believed. You are shifting into territory beyond your history. *This is where it all gets good.*

Believe me, you really do want to know just what love can do.

SELF-TRUST INQUIRY

Where are you *resisting* a situation?
How can you show up with a willingness
to move forward in a new way?
Have you had an experience of spiritual or creative surrender?

SELF-TRUST-ISMS

Instructions for Your Brave Place

I am willing to go into the black woods of any situation with one small flickering candle. I am willing—because I want to know how far self-trust will take me.

I will endure because I am worth endurance.

I don't have to believe there is a brilliant transformation at work. I just have to *be willing to believe.*

Empowerment is making our decisions from our strength instead of our pain.

The juice is in this experience, not some moment in the future. *There is something here for you.*

....

Mark this holy time in your mind. This is the border between where you've been and everything you want.

25

Siding with Your Undiluted Light

THE PRACTICE: It's time to step up your radical abilities. Go beyond your casual belief in your inner work. Know that your connection to inspired wisdom is real. Own your truth. End the weakness of waffling. Faith requires activation. **Your practice is to leap.** Refuse to listen to any voice that suggests you are naive. It requires courage and ceaseless commitment to fly.

You give the means whereby conviction comes and surety of Your abiding Love is gained at last.
—*A Course in Miracles*

The odds of your exact creation are about as likely as finding a penny on Jupiter— with Abe Lincoln face up. Heads you win. Please stop minimizing your importance.
—TAMA KIEVES, from a journal entry

It's heartbreaking to feel disconnected from ourselves. Or disconnected from our sense of well-being, the grace of feeling that our lives make sense, or are moving in a good direction. If you're human and aware, you will go through these times. It's inevitable. It's soul-wrenching and terrible. It's also workable. Yet you will have to work at staying connected to your light. You must keep gardening if you want a garden. Otherwise, the weeds win.

Years ago in a meditation, I cried out to my inner teacher, *How do I reach you?* What am I supposed to focus on? I got this message back from the deepest part of the diamond cave of my interior world: *I need you to be the beloved. Be the beloved.* Say what now?

I knew I was being asked to take my casual interest in faith and self-actualization and go deeper, go truer, and go all the way.

I knew I had to start walking forward without self-doubt. To trust in the radical love of an energy I couldn't fathom but would not deny. **I knew it meant I needed to trust myself and my life and allow it to unfold in a way that *showed me* I was guided—and that I could trust.**

I also knew I'd never see my life this way—if I didn't look for it. I had to own this birthright. I had rejected it so often. I have been suspicious of myself, poking holes in my own new tires. Yet it seems that faith requires activation. It requires engagement. *It doesn't just happen.*

Second-guessing myself wasn't helping me. It was keeping me from going deeper into my best life. Only commitment and actual experience would heal me. Self-doubt was *not* self-inquiry. Self-doubt was the rejection of my power—and of everything I *really* believed.

It was time to stop telling myself I was ineffectual. I had the edge that gave me every advantage. I wasn't limited to the perception of my reptilian brain. I possessed this secret river within me, a current of deep knowing brilliance, an energy sourced in Limitlessness. I command powerful faculties. Ernest Holmes says, "The Life of the Spirit is my life. All of Its Strength is my strength. Its Power is my power." Now I was ready to stop living as though my life were a jumble of unrelated events. I am loved by the One Presence. *Everything is loved.* It is the nature of sentience. When I dropped from my head to my heart, I could feel this nexus and knowing.

Part of me railed . . . how is believing in a "loving Universe" realistic? There is genocide, racism, blue algae in the lakes of my childhood, corrupt politicians, and global warming. And on a personal level, I had someone drop out of a class, which goes to show the Universe hates me.

Also on that personal level, I'm messy, will never have long legs, and feel vaguely threatened by AI and am afraid to type that. Sometimes I feel like I'm jetting on a spaceship for one—with despondency and anxiety as copilots . . . *and they're healthy.* How does focusing on rose petals change this?

Yet even as my inner tantrum spewed cynicism and a few truly unnecessary comments about a certain "muffin top" situation developing, I felt peaceful. Like when you know you've lost steam for an argument. Really, once you touch the truth, it's nonnegotiable.

Staying in your brain can cost too much.
Life is in the leap.

I knew that the mind could find a thousand reasons to doubt and dismiss a relationship with this energy or Loving Presence. The scientists in my head would adjust their lab coats, raise their beakers in a group anti-toast, and sneer. The business folk would pack up their sleek laptops and exit the meeting. But I knew what I knew.

Or at least on a good day I did. On a day when the marigolds were blazing orange and I had strong coffee and a breeze wafted by and the wind chimes tinkled, I knew there was an unbearable love in this world, and I wanted to serve it. I didn't need to know the name of this mystery because I knew the certainty.

I also knew that when I felt love, my doubts disappeared. This knowing reverberated like a gong. As they say, once the bell is rung, it can't be unrung. That kind of knowing feels like homecoming, a blast of well-being—the way the operating system is supposed to function. Maybe you know what I mean.

Besides, I had experience, proof of concept as they say. When I believed in something bigger, I was Rambo, baby, but with a halo, strong enough to move a grain of sand and a mountain, or to get out of bed and move past defeat. Love was the antidote to my ego's siren song of futility.

Be the beloved. I knew what this commitment asked. I would listen to my instincts more than to my defenses. Yes, there was a part of me that doubted. There was also a part of me that did not. There was a part of me *that knew I was here to thrive.* It was time to jump into the pool and swim in the goodness of this life, and not let my cynicism or practical mindedness "protect" me further.

This isn't a passive path: I take responsibility for my thoughts, and for the choices I make in every moment. Because if you believe that life can work in your favor, then you need to work in favor of yourself.

THE BELOVED IS A BADASS

Neuroscientists have shown that standing in a certain posture, the superhero pose—hands on hips and arms bent—gives us more confidence and stamina. I think of *being the beloved* as an inner version of this pose.

The beloved is someone who has decided not to be a victim in this life. You may have been hurt or degraded unfairly or make less money—and yet you will not victimize yourself. You will not take a lower role. You will rise in *any circumstance* because that is your birthright.

You are conscious. You are devoted. You will be the presence of love for yourself.

Can you imagine if you didn't ever have to experience life as trampled grass? What if you knew that *something in you* could rise again and again? That the radical presence of your guidance was unconditional—and instantaneously available? What if you could plug into a Source of dynamism that could navigate and instigate anything? You can. *You were born with these powers.*

Listen to a voice of wild divine love within you. A voice of fearless possibility. This life-force is not limited by circumstances. It is limited by your refusal to allow what you already know.

A Course in Miracles teaches that we are far too tolerant of mind wandering. We indulge our limiting thoughts. We can talk ourselves into disconnection. Sometimes our emotional wounds or traumas can hijack us into feeling alone. *You are not alone.* There is something greater going on. You did not create yourself.

Your spiritual connection is your pink diamond kiddo, the pivotal asset in your empowerment portfolio. You have the resources to metabolize pain and walk among us with astonishing powers. Your alignment and vibration can change the nature of the world you walk in. Quantum physicists have proven some funky phenomena already. This is the power of your life. It's the power of my life. And most of us have barely scratched the surface of our consciousness.

IT TAKES COURAGE TO BELIEVE
IN HIGHER POSSIBILITIES

It takes bravery to champion yourself and your inner reality. "I don't want to be a drooling idiot believing in imaginary beings," says my client Marvin, a fast-talking trial lawyer. "But then I also don't want to be an arrogant fool not using powers if I have them, especially if that's what I'm really here for." It's the sane person's dilemma. **Yet this is what an exceptional life is all about. It is the decision to embrace your maverick sensibilities. To commit to your faith instead of your fear.**

For far too long, we have been taught to "be reasonable" and measure ourselves by the world's material data instead of listening to our own instincts and the direction of our unquantifiable soul. That diminished focus is a guarantee for diminishment.

Yes, it takes power to go your own way. *But it can give you power to go your own way.* What if you could trust what you know—even when you don't know how you know it? This may be your time to tap a strength far beyond your intellectual understanding. Staying in your brain can cost too much. Life is in the leap. As poet Mark Nepo writes, "If you try to comprehend air before breathing it, you will die."

Life is a potent teacher, but you already knew that. I find that my struggles keep pushing me into more and more commitment. My lack of commitment is a gap. Fears get in through this gap and dilute my strength and progress.

I'm going to mend that gap. I will be the beloved of the Universe, and of myself. I won't let the story of myself change because of variables I do not think I like. Circumstances do not change *my identity.* I own my perspective. I own my selfhood. I own my life.

Being the beloved means not listening to any voice that denies your strength. Being the beloved means dedicating yourself to the one voice inside you that will open the gates to everything you really want. That one voice is love.

I'm going to ask you to take your rightful place here. **Side with your light, not the times you don't feel your light.** Know who you are meant to be and do not continue to demean yourself with speculations. Own your light-infused potential—your self-realized, shake-off-your-shackles-and-weep-with-gratitude potential. The world cannot stop you. The world cannot tell you who you are. You are here to tell the world who you are.

Commit to what you know within. Reject your self-rejection response. I assure you it's not naive to open to a brilliant energy and Self that is life-affirming. Look for it. Find it. Spend time cultivating this relationship. Dare to stop being so "smart" and instead crack open the full truth and power of your being.

Go all the way.

SELF-TRUST INQUIRY

What do you know about yourself or your situation
when you are siding with your light?
When have you felt connected to your Self or *guided* by love
or a bigger energy?
How could you stay more connected to your light?

SELF-TRUST-ISMS

Siding with Your Undiluted Light

Faith requires activation. It requires engagement. *It doesn't just happen.*

I needed to trust myself and my life and allow it to unfold in a way that *showed me* I was guided—and that I could trust.

Self-doubt was *not* self-inquiry. Self-doubt was the rejection of my power—and of everything I *really* believed.

I knew there was an unbearable love in this world, and I wanted to serve it.

Staying in your brain can cost too much. Life is in the leap.

Dare to stop being so "smart" and crack open the full truth and power of your being. Go all the way.

KICKSTARTS AND PRACTICES

Have at it. Play with these. Trust yourself. Go where you're guided . . .

Pick Three Self-Trust-isms from Part VI. Journal about them. Maybe make some art. Meditate or reflect on the words that spoke to you. Discuss them with someone else. Let these chosen phrases unlock a new awareness and conversation within.

1. **Resistance Recipe.** Write your recipe. Begin with compassion: How can you be kind to the part of you that is afraid? Add surrender: How can you surrender this situation to a higher love for help? Add action: What tiny step forward can you take right now?

2. **Create Your Empowerment Avatar.** Imagine and describe another part of yourself who can do anything. See this guide within you: *The One Who Can Do Anything*. Is there an image you can draw or find on Pinterest? Let this image speak to you.

3. **Your Love Leap.** Commit to your stand of believing you are *guided* and supported. Create a covenant with yourself. Mark this time with a ritual or symbolic act.

4. **Meet the Guide of Fearless Possibility.** See this guide. It asks you three questions. (1) When did you know you were strong? (2) When did you feel like anything was possible? (3) What would you do right now if you knew anything was possible? **(Enjoy my "Meet Your Strength" guided visualization for a deeper experience. It's included in your free Trust Yourself Mega Pack on page 312.)**

5. **Write Your Power Mantra.** It could be "I was born for this." Or "With love, I can do anything." Or . . . invoke a prayer or sing your mantra before a task.

6. **Keep a Miracles Log.** Write out five examples in your life of feeling supported by a benevolent energy. Times when things shifted. You met the right person. Or came upon the perfect ideas. Keep adding to your log.

PART VII

From Small-Mindedness to Selfless Love

TURNING UP THE LIGHT

THE BLOCK: Small-Mindedness
THE BREAKTHROUGH: *Selfless Love*

YOU GET IN YOUR OWN WAY
when you take actions from your smaller self.

YOU DISCOVER YOUR OWN WAY
when you act from selfless love.

Sometimes you don't trust yourself, because you are choosing from the small-mindedness of your smaller self. Your smaller self grabs for results but often feels thwarted. Your smaller self closes its pea-sized heart to life. It has "expectations" of others and circumstances—dictating limited scenarios in which you let yourself feel connected. This is a powerless way to live.

*Can you consider that it's **an attack on yourself** to hold back your greatest love?*

You grow in self-trust when you show up in selfless love. Your infinite self is here to give. You will discover who you really are when you love more.

Dare to show up in receptivity and service. Be a messenger from the realm of abundance. Your greatest healing may even come from giving what you desperately want to receive.

In this section we explore how to connect to ourselves more deeply by showing up with a giving heart and gratitude.

26

Expectations Spoil
Unexpected Love

THE PRACTICE: You block your connection to strength and love by insisting that love has to look a certain way. Your expectations of others can limit the flow of true connection. True connection emerges from nonjudgment. You may be asking someone for something they cannot give. **Your practice is to be a presence of safety and acceptance for others— and for yourself.**

*There are as many ways of loving
as there are people.*
—RUMI

*The only reason we don't open our hearts
and minds to other people is that they trigger
confusion in us that we don't feel brave
enough or sane enough to deal with.*
—PEMA CHÖDRÖN

My father is no longer alive. But when he was alive, I always had the fantasy that I would have an intimate conversation with him. He would be a bit like the *Brady Bunch* dad, cut with some Gandhi, Tony Robbins, and my favorite therapist. He'd ask me, "How would you describe the meaning of life?" Or "How can I support your essence most?" Instead, my father, a practical and private man, asked, "So, what's the population of Denver?" I'd cave with disappointment and shrug my shoulders as an answer and a rebuke.

"Delta flies over here at least twice a day," my father said, as though this were a clue to all existence. We sat together on the front porch of our house in Brooklyn where I had grown up, long before Brooklyn was cool. *I flew two thousand miles to be back home, and not on Delta, to see my parents, and this is what he wants to share with me. Flight patterns of major airlines.* I am already telling the story to all my friends in my mind. I am drowning at this point in my life and crave support. That's not what's for dinner here.

I remember railing at a therapist. Why didn't my father want to know me? Why didn't he want to "know all about me," like the song in the musical? Why didn't he love me? Why didn't he want to hear my hungers, my struggles, and my triumphs? I was his daughter, not someone he met on a bus. Why didn't he want to know my favorite memory or my worst fear?

My father *didn't* want to know details about my life. He had only one definition of success and he "didn't approve of my life-style," as he'd spit out at me more than once. Translation: I wasn't married. I wasn't married to someone Jewish. I didn't have children. I wasn't practicing law. I wasn't living in New York City. I had moved to Jupiter or Denver, Colorado, some place beyond the tri-state area. Believe you me, I hadn't even told him about the long-haired tarot card reader I was in love with at the time.

Years later, as I think about it, I suspect that my father stayed on "safe" subjects to create a Swiss neutral zone, a flying carpet between us. He was being *kind*. My father was a volatile guy who could ignite into a rage that would have had me groping in therapy for decades. A bit ahead of his time, he was on the "don't ask, don't tell, and don't yell" program. He desired a different life for me, but he still wanted to be with me.

My father also came from a generation that didn't talk about feelings. They didn't watch *Oprah* or share turning-point moments. Instead, they pulled out their wallets to show their love. My father's wallet was well-worn.

I want to tell you about the year I took my spirituality home. Not my ideology. Not my self-help slogans. This time, I brought home my willingness to heal with my father. I gave up pushing for only one scenario. I gave up my relentless need for something my father couldn't or wouldn't give me.

I lunged into the portal of what is. I decided to speak *his* language, and to stop resisting it, calling it dumb and superficial in my mind. I wasn't coming from resignation, the compliance that comes from being tired of fighting for what I couldn't get. I was making a choice. I was shifting the paradigm. I was taking my power by deciding to have mercy for my aging father, a man who did not know how to talk to his daughter but one who picked her up from the airport every single time.

Instead, on this visit home, I decide to be with him in his comfort zone instead of trying to yank him into mine. "Does United fly this way too?" I ask, as we are once again on the porch. "Does the noise ever bother you?" I tell him which airlines fly out of Denver. But I am saying, *I love you. You mean the world to me. Thank you for being my father.* And my father relaxes more. He puts his arm around me at one point. He calls me his "Black Beauty," a childhood nickname. Something flutters in my heart. It's like magic. It's like velvet. It's like love—a love that is stronger than differences or preferences.

I realized then that just as my father had been rigid in his definition of success, I had been equally rigid in my definition of love. I'd only had one door that you could come through.

All these years I'd been asking my father to do something that would have frightened or unsettled him. And true intimacy only stems from emotional safety and acceptance.

You may be asking someone for something they cannot give.

I'd been so hurt by him because he wanted me to be different. But I was doing the same thing to him: I wanted him to be different.

My father and I had always butted heads. We both liked to have things our own way. We subscribed to the "my way or the highway" school of life. But that year I took the high road instead of the highway. I extended an olive branch instead of swacking him across the head with one and calling it a desire for connection.

It wasn't the conversation I'd always dreamed about, but our conversation was a love poem when you looked beyond the words into the exchange. I was saying: "I accept you. I bless you. I thank you." He was saying: "I know. Thank you. I've always loved you. I'm so happy to have you here."

My father died a few years later. I am forever grateful for the spiritual work I'd done to stretch and respond to my life and to him from love instead of screaming need. It was a miracle. It was an experience of realizing my highest potential. *I liked who I was in that situation.* For me, that's the point of healing and growing. We discover the exhilarating freedom of personal power. **We don't have to lose our connection to love and strength because of what someone else does or doesn't do.**

You get to choose the frequency you bring into every room. You get to decide how you want to show up, who you want to be in this lifetime. It has nothing to do with what others are choosing to do. Others might be frightened. They may have regrets. They may criticize or feel embittered. You don't have to see yourself through their eyes.

You also get to choose how you see others—and here's a hint. You will benefit most by choosing not to judge the hell out of them. **Be the one who loves. You don't have to see their mistakes or faltering as their destiny and identity.** Everyone is shifting and growing, even when they seem stuck. Nothing in this life will ever stay the same. Please don't decide you know who someone is. Don't lock them into a coffin of definition or one well-rehearsed memory. Don't lock yourself into that dark room either.

Of course, I will make this distinction. I am not saying you need to tolerate all behaviors. I am not saying you can't have standards. I am never saying you should remain with someone who abuses you or harms you. Always listen to your guidance.

For the rest of your situations, you might want to try this practice of love. (And out of self-love, if you're feeling a bit Genghis Khan–ish, give Mother Teresa a raincheck. You have the right and responsibility to go at your own pace.) Walk into your office or your mother's house or even a room from the past in your imagination, with the intention of having compassion or being the presence of love.

Be a stand for kindness. Be a messenger. Or a tuning fork that allows others to remember what is right in themselves and in this life. You don't even have to like the person. You don't have to ask them out to lunch. You don't even have to see them again. Do stop judging them, attacking them in your head. For your sake, not for theirs.

Say in your mind: *I accept you just as you are right now. I want you to feel safe in this moment. Thank you for everything good you have done in this lifetime.* Notice how the room begins to soften and the person before you relaxes as though a weight has lifted. You have no idea the good that this can do.

Your brother-in-law, coworkers, or sister may be different from you, but the need for love is always the same. Your need to remain true to your light in every situation is also the same. Let go of some of your expectations and experience the liberation of love.

SELF-TRUST INQUIRY

Think about someone in your life you wish would be different.
What expectation do you have of him or her?
How else could you show up?

~

SELF-TRUST-ISMS

Expectations Spoil Unexpected Love

You may be asking someone for something that they cannot give.

I'd been so hurt by him because he wanted me to be different. But I was doing the same thing to him: I wanted him to be different.

We don't have to lose our connection to love and strength because of what someone else does or doesn't do.

You don't have to see their mistakes . . . as their destiny and identity.

Please don't decide you know who someone is. Don't lock them into a coffin of definition or one well-rehearsed memory.

Be a stand for kindness . . . Or a tuning fork that allows others to remember what is right in themselves.

27

The Joy of Giving Wildly

THE PRACTICE: Sometimes we let go of our smaller selves by giving our love to someone else. As we give, we receive. When we give, we summon forth the gifts and strength we have. We own it. We become who we have always wanted to be. You may be called to give in ways that surprise you. **Your practice is to answer the invitation to help someone else.**

No one has ever become poor from giving.
—ANNE FRANK

All that I give is given to myself.
—*A Course in Miracles*

We are all love-seeking individuals brainwashed to believe that love is somewhere else. The truth is we are lovers. We are the witch doctors. We are the shamans. We have the power to heal ourselves and bring everyone around us closer to infinite good.

I want to tell you about one of the proudest highlights of my life.

I'm not going to tell you how I led an amazing spiritual retreat or did a TEDx Talk. I'm going to tell you about the day I helped my eighty-two-year-old mother clean out a closet. For me, it was a time out of time, an experience when I dropped to my knees in the river of the real. Yeah, I drank the Kool-Aid. Hell, I mixed up another batch.

Let me back up a bit, to give this story context.

I have had a mixed relationship with my mother in this lifetime. I know my mother loved me the best she could. But I have also had a hard time with her. My mother wasn't all that into mothering. There were no chocolate chip cookies baked, no special notes in my book bag, no stories to help me grow. My mother didn't teach me to believe in myself, or failing that, to tweeze my eyebrows.

In some ways my mother was a child who never grew up. I often have a vision of her as stuck as a thirteen-year-old girl, unconsciously mean. She would say cutting things about others. "Would you look at that outfit, who would wear that?" she would say loudly. Or "Look at that fat schlub."

Mind you, I am a former anorexic, but that didn't slow my mother down for a second from judging women's body types. My mother was not aware or concerned about the needs of others, even if you communicated carefully and nonjudgmentally, just like your therapist taught you to do. Even if you shrieked them, just like your therapist taught you not to do.

There are reasons, of course. My mother didn't have a kind mother, no one to guide her or wipe her chin in this life. I've found that kind of love beyond my biological family. And some of my healing has come in giving to my mother what I desperately wanted to receive. Yes, read that line again. I'll wait.

Getting back to the story. I'd flown in to teach at the New York Open Center in the garment district of New York City. The next day I hoped to see my mother, who lived more than ninety minutes away. When you live across the country, everything seems close by if it's in the same state.

My brother couldn't bring my mother into the city to see me. He had plans. His wife wanted him to go to the mall. Something like that. And my mother wouldn't take a train in by herself, though she did it for other things. I began spiraling down the rabbit hole of feeling insignificant to my family.

Then, I don't even remember how, but an idea came to me: *If they won't come to the city, you could go upstate to see your mother.* Yes, I only had a few hours before I had to get to JFK Airport and catch a flight home to Denver. Yes, it would involve a cab ride and a ninety-minute train ride to my mother's house. Then I'd have to make the same exact trip in reverse and get to JFK to catch my four-hour flight back to Denver, all in the same day. I *could* do it. I *could* have a few hours with my mother.

It was crazy, I thought. Still this kundalini energy or something wild awoke within me. I *could* do this. I have crazy stamina, especially when I'm inspired. I could see my mother. I didn't have to be a victim of circumstances. I was not helpless. I could be outrageous. I could swim the English Channel or take a train. I would be the game-show host of my own life. Nothing could stop me. I had the power to do it, and I would.

My mother looked at me in disbelief in the Beekman Square Diner. I slurped my chicken matzoh ball soup, a luxury sparely available in Denver. "What did you come up here for?" she said. I smiled and said, "I came to see you." She didn't say anything. The question hung midair. *Why would you do that?* She couldn't believe that anyone would make any effort, much less intense effort, just to be with her. "I wanted to be with you," I said again. I was hoping she'd feel like a princess.

We only had an hour and a half back in my mother's condo.

My mother had lived in a brand-new space since my father died. She loved having this place. Yet over time, some of her old habits had caught up with her. She showed me her cluttered closet, a closet too small to hold the frenzy of her lust. She had taken to shopping as a sport. She was a child set free from the domination of my father. And she had her own credit card. She loved going to the mall, and she had also fallen in love with ordering from mail-order catalogs.

"I thought this would go with these green pants," she said, holding up a tunic-type garment with bold stripes and ornate buttons. "Or I could wear it with these pants." She pulled out other ensembles, snazzy affairs, and I wondered where she would wear them in her condo complex of retirees, men and women who wore velour sweat suits and thick white sneakers.

My mother loved clothes and as she brought out more outfits, she seemed to me like a little girl that was showing me her Barbie's clothes. Barbie goes to dinner on a cruise. Barbie goes to coffee klatch. Barbie visits her son, who maybe doesn't see her enough.

Her closet was packed, clothes stuffed in like stowaways and immigrants on the lower level of the ships you see in old movies. My heart hurt as I looked at this.

I felt bad because my own closets were starting to go the same way, and I'd felt shame about it. My mother had scarcity issues and I'd followed her model. I held on to shirts from former decades and identities, or pants of hopeful sizes. I was always reinventing myself. My closet looked as though several women lived there. Several women with varying emotional states of well-being.

I'd always judged my mother's closets. I blamed them for my own. She had not taught me pride in neatness. She had not taught me organization or how to let anything go. She did not trust life. She clung to everything. I looked at her offending closet and winced.

Then, I had this wild idea. Like, outrageous. Wilder than the decision to travel upstate to see her. To this day, I don't know how it happened. Maybe the angel Michael or some advanced cosmic entity whispered in my ear. As I looked at the despicable closet, **I decided I wanted to help her instead of judge her.** I wanted to show up with love, ferocious love. "Let's clean your closet out," I said. My mother's face dropped. "Oh no," she said automatically. The hoarder within her bared its teeth.

We let go of our smaller selves by giving our love to someone else.

I immediately shifted into a part of myself I really love. It's the part of myself that coaches other people. That part has patience and conviction and knows that her love will take on any shape or form and will find a way through. I spoke gently to my mother. "We'll just do this one item at a time," I said. "I mean it. You can tell me to stop at any time, and I will."

I pulled out a big blouse that I knew didn't fit her and it was a loud number to boot, oranges and purples. "How about this?" I said, and we both giggled. "Can you part with this? I know it's so you and all. I know this is probably your best look." We both laughed and she nodded. I threw this first victim on the carpet. Soon there would be a mountain of fabric that later we stuffed into bags and donated to Goodwill on the way to the train station.

I continued with obvious choices. A tent of a dress. Okay. I moved on to shirts that had color repetitions. Say, five olive-green shirts. "Can you let go of one of these?" I watched her slump and pick at a nail. "You don't have to do anything, Ma. It's okay. I am only going to listen to you. I'm not going to judge you for anything. But I don't know that you'd miss this one shirt." In truth, she didn't know she had it. It had crumpled into the back of the closet, the Bermuda triangle, a place where clothes would never be heard from again.

"Okay," she said, and into the pile it went. We went on like this for the time we had. "This is what you want to do with your time?" she said to me, and it was. I wanted her to feel loved. I wanted her to feel taken care of. When I first met Paul, my partner, he had taken care of me. He would be patient and loving and help me do unthinkable things, like hang up pictures, clean out drawers, get things organized. It felt like having a private angel. My mother didn't have any angels. I wanted her to have the experience that I had had.

The time zipped past. I hung everything back up. We had made that one small closet functional and friendly, and it was a work of art. We both stared at it like it was the *Mona Lisa*. Or like something from television.

I felt high. I mean really high, like I had just come out of the desert having sung the earth alive with a medicine man. My mother and I drove to Pawling, where she waited with me for the Metro North train to Grand Central.

I felt so alive on that train, even though I knew I had major travel hours ahead of me. Then I met three spirited young men going into New York City to a friend's bar and one thing led to another and we ended up singing "New York, New York" together on the train. And this pretty much completed the larger-than-life day I had given myself.

Bewitchment took place that day. I had stepped out of my usual character in the play. I played the good mother. I played the awesome daughter. I played the kind human being. I played someone with power: a woman who acted independently and didn't have to be triggered and resentful. This was my true potential. All our true potential. That day, I was the good wolf in the Native American stories, the one you feed if you want to save the world.

No, I wasn't being a martyr. Or indulging a savior complex.

I was inspired. I couldn't make that feeling happen. But it happened, and it felt good. Over time I transformed my relationship with my mother. I realized I was the mother in this situation. It really didn't work any other way.

I had once written in my journal in anger: *Why do I have to be the nurturing one? Why can't she want to take care of me? Why do I have to be the one who doesn't judge and who shows up with kindness?* And the voice of love said this to me in meditation: *Whoever is stronger in the lifetime will be the one who loves more.* And that was that.

This call to love helped me step out of the shackles of expectations. It helped me step out of the slavery of "what should be" and wasn't. I had a life of resources. I'd taken my ragged pain to therapists and friends and lovers. I had healed. I was stronger in the lifetime.

My mother died close to a year after. I often think back to cleaning her closet. It is one of the best things I have ever done with my life.

There are a lot of spiritual traditions that teach us that to give is to receive. Sometimes when you first see a principle like that, especially when you're feeling fragile, it seems like a bad idea. It seems like you're adding insult to injury. Like you've been hurt, and now, you're the one who is being asked to buy cupcakes for others. It's preposterous to your ego. It's empowering to your soul.

A word about giving: giving is not meant to be mechanical or puritanical. A call to give is a customized invitation. You will feel drawn. Compelled. Enabled.

The power of giving may surprise you, as your own mystical energy stirs to life. **When we give, it's like plugging in to the Source. We realize we are more than who we think we are.** The crazy thing is that while you're giving to someone else, you're really giving to a part of yourself. I can tell you, *I* felt nurtured as I nurtured my mother.

We all heal our wounds and let go of our smaller selves in our own way. Some people do a shamanic journey and battle in the underworld with a slithering sea creature with amber eyes and poison fangs. Others join the Peace Corps or adopt a child or interpret their dreams on leather couches with Jungian analysts. I rode a few trains upstate and cleaned my mother's closet.

SELF-TRUST INQUIRY

As you read this, is there someone you might
like to help in some way?
If you were being outrageously generous, what might you do?

SELF-TRUST-ISMS

The Joy of Giving Wildly

We let go of our smaller selves by giving our love to someone else.

I didn't have to be a victim of circumstances . . . I could be outrageous. I could swim the English Channel or take a train.

I wanted to help her instead of judge her.

Why do I have to be the one who doesn't judge . . . And the voice of love said this . . . *Whoever is stronger in the lifetime will be the one who loves more.*

....

When we give, it's like plugging in to the Source. We realize we are more than who we think we are.

....

The crazy thing is that while you're giving to someone else, you're really giving to a part of yourself.

28

Broken People Make
Great Trailblazers

The Practice: When you leave behind your "little self" you become an instrument of grace. Pain is a gateway into your healing powers. Your "limitation" can become what marketers call your origin story. To heal your struggle, you will stretch into your light and highest capacities. **Your practice is to use your pain to expand—instead of victimizing yourself in any way.** Then you have the opportunity to help others. Your pain becomes a gift.

Obstacles are another way that spirit calls my name. Obstacles push me to discover a new identity, one that is not limited by this obstacle.
—TAMA KIEVES, from a journal entry

Make of yourself a light.
—THE BUDDHA

Sometimes I don't want to be a light. I'd rather aim a little lower in life. Maybe figure out how to numb my consciousness instead of raise it. I don't need to be a saint. Let better people have at it. Yet *A Course in Miracles* teaches that doing your inner work is not optional. There is only one way home.

Since we are living in semi-chaotic times, as though someone is shaking up the snow globe, and times that can sometimes even feel dark, I want to talk to you about light—your light.

A Course in Miracles teaches, "I am the light of the world. That is my only function. That is why I am here." When I first read that line, part of me stood at attention as though its true name had been called through the mist and disorientation of a thousand years. The other part of me felt screwed.

I had been so hoping to be rescued. Then I thought if I was the light of the world, humanity was in a pickle. After all, I had journals filled with rant-ish rambles and a desire to run for the hills. Humanity deserved a more impressive guide.

We are all called. Thank goodness light doesn't require perfection, and "issues" are part of our function. My limitations have been my personal trainers, pushing me into a conscious relationship with myself and my truth. I've found the greatest solutions *because* I had problems.

Through facing fear and uncertainty, I did the best thing I have ever done in my life. I began this enigmatic, compelling relationship with my inner teacher. I found a wavelength of continuous clarity. I grew a thousand feet tall with a heart pumping oxygen as fresh as clover, or it sure felt that way on some occasions. Yes, limitations put pins in my couch and lumps in my pillow—so that I could not fall asleep to my true potential.

"Limitations" also gave me an unassailable credential in this world. My life's work arose from my trials. I wouldn't have become a voice for others without them. I assumed my place among the wounded healers and the phoenixes. I've never been a "talking head" leader or coach. I am all in, teaching what I'm practicing. Challenges keep my feet to the fire.

I know what it's like to be in the pit. Hell, it's indeed possible that I am in another pit, even if I'm keynoting in front of an audience of a thousand people. I will never stop growing and walking out of my own thought prison. This is why I can remind others that they will not stay stuck. I'm not waiting until I'm "perfect" to help people. I know I am not my limitations, even when I have limitations.

> *My limitations have been my personal trainers . . . I have found the greatest solutions <u>because</u> I had problems.*

Yes, I know, you don't always feel as though you have it together. Trust me on this. **We who are questioning our lives and our abilities are the light of the world. We will be beacons of comfort, hope, and direction to those who need us. We are in the soup, but it is healing broth.**

It's okay to flounder. We are the ones who are learning to find freedom in the middle of societal pressures, anxieties, or just your garden-variety freak-show conditions. This is heroic. This is damn amazing.

Our world is changing. The old ways are falling apart. Some talk about being in a revolutionary evolution of consciousness. We are the ones. We are the ones who are discovering our sacred resources and responses and bringing them to the table. We are the ones who raise the standards of what's possible. Or dance with our loved ones in our kitchens, even as the stock market falters—because we know a security that does not waiver.

Our dark days and stumbles are our training grounds. We are learning how to recognize a grace that is never threatened in any way. A love that is never far away. We are discovering the underground, cool sweet waters in what seems to be an endless desert. We are the ones.

Your pain is your guru in disguise. How do you show up for this guru? How do you resist the urge to curse your discomfort, or just order a thousand Domino's pizzas and have a nice, dysfunctional affair with the delivery boy for toppings? How do you sit down right now—and trust the strange perfection of where you are? What if your struggle isn't meaningless? What if it's your light breaking through? What if you could choose to stay with it and expand—and know that your journey is valuable to the rest of us? You can. This is your assignment. You are the light of the world.

I don't think a life of freedom is about creating a fortress of iron-clad conditions, imagining you will never deal with uncertainty again. A life of self-trust is about awakening to your higher Self, a source of love and fluency with all of life. You yearn to feed the wild blue bird in your heart on berries not of this world—so that you will move through any circumstance with agility. Believe me, you want connection more than you want protection. Yes, you do have a blue bird in your heart. No, you should not repeat this to others.

I don't wish suffering on anyone. Yet pain is part of the bells and whistles of being human. Might as well as use it. Might as well become the light of the world. The oyster produces a pearl through the irritation of sand. Peacocks grow their iridescent feathers by eating thorns. "What is to give light must endure burning," wrote Viktor Frankl, the famous Holocaust survivor and psychiatrist. And Buddhist nun Pema Chödrön says, "Only to the extent that we expose ourselves over and over to annihilation can that which is indestructible in us be found."

We may not have easy lives at this moment. But it's not because we're falling short or damaged. It's because our souls demand expansion. We are evolving. Moving from coping with what is to changing the story of our lives and the story of the world.

We are the teachers, healers, visionaries, social entrepreneurs, and architects of the new day. We are the sensitive ones, the canaries in the mines. **Maybe we have never been fit for this world. That's exactly why we are the ones who can transform the world.**

I like to imagine that there's this whole mystical butterfly effect taking place—and that as any one of us finds our way out of a paper bag, then all of us begin to strut in the light. Scientists coined the term "butterfly effect" to explain how a butterfly flapping its wings in South America can change the wind current and alter a tornado's location in Oklahoma. It's that whole interconnectedness thing. That's why when one of us heals our pain—even in the tiniest way—we brighten the collective. And someone in Walmart stops yelling.

We will turn darkness into hope, as humanity has always done. We will exemplify that pain passes and leaves strength and vision in its wake. We may write screenplays or paint murals that open hearts and minds. We may usher in paradigm shifts in business, healthcare, or education. We may organize a nonprofit, do yoga with veterans, or forgive someone in our lives. We might simply say hello to our neighbor.

We are in the study halls now. We are squirming and sweating through self-mastery. Some of us have listened to a thousand podcasts. Others have calluses on their butts from meditation.

We are the ones who are confronting our inner pain and opening to a larger life. We are turning this hurt into abundance for everyone. Jesus is said to have demonstrated miracles and walked on water. We are doing something miraculous and challenging in our times. We are healing and walking in this world.

SELF-TRUST INQUIRY

What is your pain teaching you?
How might you benefit someone else with what you are learning?

———⌣———

SELF-TRUST-ISMS

Broken People Make Great Trailblazers

....

We are all called. Thank goodness light doesn't require perfection, and "issues" are part of our function.

....

My limitations have been my personal trainers ... I've found the greatest solutions *because* I had problems.

....

Limitations put pins in my couch and lumps in my pillow—so that I could not fall asleep to my true potential.

....

I'm not waiting until I'm "perfect" to help people. I know I am not my limitations, even when I have limitations.

....

Trust me, you want connection more than you want protection.

....

Maybe we have never been fit for this world. That's exactly why we are the ones who can transform the world.

29

A Life Practice of Abundance

THE PRACTICE: Your smaller self may be desperate to receive. Perhaps you feel this lack in your life because you are numb. You do not long for things or events as much as you long to feel your Self again. You ache to feel alive and awake. Only love awakens you. Gratitude activates love. **Your practice is to thank yourself and the Universe—frequently—for everything you have already received.**

The root of joy is gratefulness.
—DAVID STEINDL-RAST

The quantum field responds not to what we want; it responds to who we are being.
—JOE DISPENZA

The self-help culture is a firehose of possibility. It tells us we're unlimited, yay! Yet if the world is your oyster . . . do you ever feel like it's snapped shut or locked with a combination lock—and you have the wrong numbers?

Maybe you don't have "all the great things" that supposedly your limitless potential could create. You don't even have one little Manhattan penthouse. Your life still has cracks in the walls. You feel more like a dud than a genie.

I remember reading the enticing information of how we can attract or manifest money, love, travel, health, and more, more, more. Who doesn't love hearing that? Well, me, after a while. I couldn't help but secretly wonder—why, oh, why then don't *I* have a country home in Tuscany or just Woodstock, New York? A trust fund or patron? A million engaged followers on social media?

What am I doing wrong? Am I in some outpost or underworld where the laws of attraction don't reach? Does some supreme being just slightly detest me? What thought am I thinking that holds back my spillage of treasure? Or is thinking you can leverage your good with your mind just magical superstition?

I'm no expert in quantum physics, but I do know this. I have never connected to happiness or a current of universal inspiration by looking at *what I don't have.* It is only my smaller self that thinks it needs better and better circumstances to feel better. The dog chasing its tail, a frustrating game.

Grasping is the booby prize. Receiving is where it's at. Your love is strong and infinite, and no circumstance can give you what you already have. How can you begin receiving the exact grace that is already in your life? That's the only question that matters. This is what I've learned on my journey of trusting myself. When I appreciate myself and my life, I see how blessed I am now. *I am the beloved.* I am a rock star plugged into an amp and, baby, the light show has begun.

Our smaller selves are always trying to get somewhere. But Eckhart Tolle, and the Buddha before him, tell us that now is where the treasure is. Now is where Spirit hangs out, with kaleidoscopic perspective, just waiting to make you cry out with wild gratitude. **When we take in the good of our own lives,** *the immensity of what we have already been given,* **we expand naturally.** Our energy plumps up like a fat, happy succulent plant in sunshine. We're not hungry anymore. We already have what we came for. And now we are lightning rods, irresistibly attractive.

Grasping is the booby prize.
Receiving is where it's at.

I want to tell you about the gratitude miracle I experienced while on a vacation in Thailand. I went from asking to have my desires met to having them met in just one day. But it's not how you might think. This is a wild gratitude story and a teaching that I am still unpacking and integrating into my life. Yes, because it's that good.

ASKING TO HAVE MY DESIRES MET

The first thing I noticed in Bangkok besides the beastly heat were the shrines everywhere, elaborate spirit houses, some the size of a bureau, others the size of a flowerpot. I saw one at a gas station, one in front of a mall, and even a tiny one the size of a matchbox hanging from the rearview mirror of my taxi driver's cab.

I decided that these mini shrines were altars. And in the fervor of someone who has just begun a trip halfway across the world, I resolved to step into conscious communication with myself and life. I decided that each time I saw a shrine on the street, I would set an intention for something I desired in my life.

Then I'd surrender this desire to the big kahuna of infinite love and transformation and know that it would be lifted, purified, and transmuted, no matter how muddled my desire or how thick the air felt. Believe me, the air was as thick as an elephant. So was my mind.

My new practice grew. I chose to think about a different aspect of my life each time I saw one of these shrines. At one altar I prayed for help with my business, asking for expansion. At another altar, I prayed for health for myself and my partner, family, friends, the world. I owned the desire I had, and I also asked for help. This felt all "spiritual" because I was being aware multiple times a day instead of once in the morning during meditation, and then getting hoovered into the blur of the day.

A lovely practice, but it wasn't my big shift. I didn't really have a miracle until I went to Chiang Mai's Sunday night bazaar just beyond the Tha Pae Gate. No, it wasn't just the great bargains for luggage, art, food, and silk shirts. Though that did sort of loosen up my chakras.

I was looking at a table covered in artsy magnets, images of elephants, bicycles, and the word "Thailand" in every color. *What magnet do I want to hang on my fridge in Denver?* I thought. Suddenly I wanted to write about the notion that I was choosing my memory of Thailand—*while in Thailand*—and sending it to my future self, and how, perhaps, I was always deciding my experiences in this way. Then I began to cry.

It wasn't the idea that had moved me to my core. It was the fact that I'd *had* an idea, because I'd been going through a long drought within myself, feeling dead and unable to care about anything or to write. I'd secretly hoped that maybe coming to Thailand would help me find a door to my creative instincts or life energy again. Looking at those magnets, I'd felt a droplet of rain inside myself, a wisp of inspiration.

I felt my best friend, my sacred companion, return to me, just like the first day the sun warms your skin after a cold spell, and you remember what it's like to feel loved. I'd thought I'd never feel this special presence again. I wanted to weep. I wanted to write.

I was back, connected to homecoming. I could taste the moon again, like all poets do. I was awake.

Then I saw a gorgeous temple right across the street. Seriously. Then again, there may have been a temple across every street there. "I have to go in there," I said to Paul, my travel mate, who didn't miss a beat and rushed in with me.

We slipped off our shoes, and I scurried to the front. I sat before this huge golden Buddha, practically the size of a Burger King. As I meditated there, this instant hit of love shot through my veins. I was high on my creative moment back at the magnet stand. I was high on the fact that I was in Thailand. I was high on the thought that I was doing what I'd always said I'd do someday. I was dedicating myself to listening to myself, to my sweet Self, to my wholeness. I was so grateful to feel alive again. I felt like I'd already gotten what I came for, no matter how the rest of the trip unfolded.

This gratitude rushed through me like a triumphant river flooding its banks. I was alive. *Thank you*. I was here. *Thank you*. I am a writer. *Thank you*. *I will be your writer,* I said to God, to Spirit, to anyone who would listen—and to that huge, golden Buddha who had absorbed the energy of thousands who had been in this temple.

A deep silence of eternal forgiveness permeated the air. I felt like the top of my head was very thin, a light membrane, maybe like a crocheted yarmulke that still let the light in, a vast Universe above and all around me. *I will serve,* I said inside myself. I am so grateful for the gift of being creative and being alive. *Thank you. Thank you. Thank you.*

Just then, I had another thought. Because one good, inspired thought often births another.

EXPERIENCING THE FULFILLMENT OF MY DESIRES

I realized I didn't want to stop along the altars of Thailand and *ask* for things. I wanted to stop along the altars of Thailand and *offer thanks*. I wanted to offer thanks everywhere, for what I was already receiving and what I already had. I would offer thanks for the health I did have, this day, this moment, never mind the future and what could be.

I could offer thanks for the money I did have. I could offer thanks for the creative instincts I did have. And in offering thanks I'd be receiving, right then and there. I wouldn't be straining for gains or grains. I'd be taking in all that was mine already. I'd be metabolizing nutrients instead of starving. I'd be loving my life instead of making mental lists of where it might improve.

In appreciating the specifics of my life, I'd grow that energy. I know enough to know that perception changes everything. Like attracts like. Lack calls lack. Begging calls more begging. *Receiving calls forth more receiving.*

I saw how casually ungrateful I'd been, an entitled tourist in the Universe, traipsing through the kingdom, demanding new treats when I hadn't even taken in the kindness and abundance all around me. There is always kindness in our midst. There is always something to appreciate.

I had taken the generosity of this life for granted. I had asked for "more" from a state of numbness or even resentment. But I realized then that it was not "more" that I needed. I needed to be awake. I wanted to be alive. *I want to feel my life. I want to receive my life.* When I'm connected to feeling myself and blessing myself, I really do want to thank my life for absolutely everything.

Maybe you do too. I hope so.

SELF-TRUST INQUIRY

In this moment, what would you like to thank
the Universe and yourself for?
If there's an area in your life where you feel lack—
what can you be grateful for in that same area?

SELF-TRUST-ISMS

A Life Practice of Abundance

I have never connected to happiness or a current of universal inspiration by looking at *what I don't have.*

Grasping is the booby prize. Receiving is where it's at.

Your love is strong and infinite, and no circumstance can give you what you already have.

In offering thanks . . . I'd be loving my life instead of making mental lists of where it might improve.

Lack calls lack. Begging calls more begging. *Receiving calls forth more receiving.*

When I'm connected to feeling myself and blessing myself, I really do want to thank my life for absolutely everything.

KICKSTARTS AND PRACTICES

Have at it. Play with these. Trust yourself. Go where you're guided . . .

Pick Three Self-Trust-isms from Part VII. Journal about them. Maybe make some art. Meditate or reflect on the words that spoke to you. Discuss them with someone else. Let these chosen phrases unlock a new awareness and conversation within.

1. **See the World from Their Eyes.** Consider a challenging relationship. How does this person see the world? What do they want from you? What might be going on for them? Journal about it. Draw a cartoon of stick figures with thought bubbles.

2. **Expectations Inventory.** Draw two columns. In one column list the people you are in a relationship with. In the next column, write out your secret scripts for each person. How do you "need" them to be? *Decide to let go of your scripts.*

3. **Turn Your Pain Into Purpose.** Write a letter of empathy and suggestions to an imaginary reader. Consider starting a support group or becoming an activist.

4. **Imagine Meeting the Guide of Selfless Love.** Breathe in boundless energy. This guide asks you three questions. (1) What does it feel like when you've received love? (2) What would it feel like to be generous and

SMALL-MINDEDNESS TO SELFLESS LOVE   297

feel a love coming through you? (3) Who might you
want to serve?

5. **Craft Your Gratitude Mantra.** Or use this one: "I am
grateful for myself in this moment because . . . *[fill in
the blank].*" Pick three regular daily times (like when
you brush your teeth) to say this.

6. **Your Outrageous Give.** What can you do as a crazy
act of generosity? If you could empower or help
someone in any way—what would you do? Try it!

PART VIII

The End Is
the Beginning

HERE WE GO!

30

Two Practices to Help You Continue Trusting Yourself

Self-trust is the first secret of success.
—RALPH WALDO EMERSON

Trusting ourselves—and our lives—doesn't just happen in the blink of an eye. You will be in constant conversation with your life. And in some moments, life will push you up against the wall like a thug in an alley on a dark night in the rain—just when you were beginning to dream about visiting Paris.

I care about you. I would hate for a time of discouragement to stop you from trusting your path. Let's talk. You are going to have days when you don't feel like a champion of the possible. You will feel like a dead rat, a tired, middle-aged victim of the probable, a limp noodle, and as though you are hanging by a thread. Hey, you amazing light—you are still on track.

Because often we learn to trust ourselves and our lives by facing the things that challenge us. I so wish there was an easier system. Or someone you could pay to do the grunt work. But it's not like that. Not only do we need to brave things, but we need to *keep braving them.* I guess it's like exercise. Just when you think you've sweated enough and that you deserve to stop now for the rest of your life, some perky, fit trainer tells you, "It's a way of life," which can sound like awful news.

We strengthen our self-trust muscles by daring to do things that make us doubt ourselves. In yoga, when you have mastered a position, you take it up a notch. You intensify the pose. Learning to trust yourself and your higher resources is like this too. We face new situations where we don't yet have confidence. We show up. That's how we grow our track record and a faith that sustains us to do anything we desire.

Remember, you are a ninja. Your challenges make you a ninja. Grow—or lose ground. Yes, dedication is gnarly. Maybe you feel like you just don't want to bother. Yet I promise you this. The results of dedication are sublime, which is why I'm reminding you to *always* bother.

I offer you two simple practices, and they will help you be there for yourself no matter what.

PRACTICE # 1: BE KIND TO YOU

Sometimes you will feel as though nothing is working, and you can't hear an inner voice of love. Everything good and true seems far away, a distant memory like a tree of cherry blossoms on a hillside you once saw in childhood, or while stoned at a party. The cherry blossoms are real. The goodness of life is still here pulsing with new chances, always new chances.

Your wise Source continues to accompany you, even when you're feeling alone. Yes, you may think you're all on your own except for your anxieties and other hounds of hell. You are just closed off from the truth. You are not experiencing the truth.

Be kind to you. The energy of kindness changes everything.

The *experience of love*—not the quoting of memes and philoso-phies. **How can you be kind to yourself right now?**

There are times when I feel stuck and *dark,* and I don't want to work to change my thoughts. I won't lift a pinkie. I'm not going to read a self-help book (or write one), sit down to meditate, jour-nal, or say that nifty nervous-system-regulating affirmation I saw on YouTube. In fact, I am going to judge the woman who posted it because she is a thin, adorable blonde, and you get where I'm going with this.

I will sulk in my swampland for as long as it takes for the emotion to run through me. I know that I'm probably messing up my energy field and polluting the collective consciousness for everyone. Am I trusting myself? Nope. Am I trusting in higher resources? Nah. Here's what I am trusting: the thought that I will never come out of this. These feelings feel so real.

And if you ever feel this way, stuck or falling way down the well, I have four words for you: be kind to you.

There are times when you just have to stop resisting where you are. The light isn't in thinking only "positive thoughts." The light is in remembering to be loving to ourselves no matter where we are.

Be kind to you. Don't give yourself a pep talk or a sermon. Give yourself a break. Put honey in your tea. Drink the apple juice of acceptance.

Have you ever been in a place where you're struggling, and someone says something all pink taffy to you like, "Everything happens for a reason," and you want to scream until you shatter glass, platitudes, and maybe their eardrums? Maybe that's just me.

Their advice might even be "right." But it's the wrong time. Or it's flippant or preachy. It's just not loving to insist on the kind of positivity that doesn't see human grief or sadness as positive. Real love sees *everything* with love. Real love trusts the process.

Allow yourself to be where you are. Please don't pressure yourself to be instantaneously connected to the bright forces within. It's okay to hurt. Self-acceptance *is* positive. Be kind to you.

PRACTICE # 2: CHOOSE AGAIN

When you're ready, begin again. Choose again. You possess the ability to give yourself a new chance. Life is always, *always* giving you a new chance.

Sometimes you need to sit down and let things be. But then you need to choose again. In yoga practice, there is Child's Pose, a soft resting pose for when things get too difficult. It's a pose of integration or reset. Those who practice yoga don't shun Child's Pose. It's an essential tool. We also don't *live* in Child's Pose. We don't give up on trying.

We rest and then we rise. This is the practice for your journey too. Sometimes you need to cry. Or let anger snap, crackle, and pop. We are human and it serves us to honor all dimensions of our experience. Yet we are also spiritual warriors. We know that there is no happiness in holding on to states of mind that hold us back. We know that only moving forward teaches us who we really are.

Begin again. When you fall off the wagon of your own faith or progress, it's time to *choose again* to trust yourself. Begin this moment. The minute you start, *you begin to win.*

If you were trusting yourself, what would you do now?
If you were trusting your Self, what would you feel now?

Every second is a doorway. You can walk straight into a new life. Choose again. Be your own phoenix rising. Stay conscious. Empower your strength more than your doubts.

Love always has another solution, perspective, or ace in the hole. There is always more love coming down the pike. Begin again.

Trusting yourself is a perpetual devotion and inspired-life-practice.

I am so very proud of you. Please know this: it's working. Every second you spend developing a deeper relationship with yourself, it's working. You are beloved. You are resourced. You are moving in alignment toward that which will align you even more. You have the guidance of an infinitely intelligent Presence, streaming through the filter of your intuition and your heart's desires. This life of yours is a wonder.

Stop wondering.

Start trusting.

Then let your magic take you everywhere you are meant to be.

31

My Tiny Little Epilogue

Writing this book has been a labor of love—and a little bit like putting a puzzle together, which seems to be impossible until suddenly some of the pieces grow wings, fly into the stratosphere, reveal their true shapes, then land where they always belonged. Can you say awe? I can.

I kept writing, imagining that someone—maybe you—would read my words and begin to *really know* you have a wise internal source. I pictured my words slipping past your societal conditioning and picking all the tiny combination locks within you. Then your answers and direction would course through you undiluted. This kept me writing. No pressure here, but I also envisioned that you have formidable gifts and compassion to give the world, and it seems like we could use you. I hope you'll get to it.

This is my sixth book. Part of me wanted to figure out what to write that would sell. I wish my guidance would focus more on things like visibility for my work or the bottom line, but it always seems to care more about healing me as I write. This is so annoying.

It makes sense, of course. If I am going to guide you in any way, I have to go first. I dug deep for this book, looking at my own pain and anxieties. I looked at what had worked for me and what hadn't. I didn't want to pretend to be an expert that had it all together. Besides, I could never pull that off. It would be exhausting and serve no one.

I'm still learning to trust myself, follow my instincts, especially when it feels as though the stakes are higher. Like clients and participants in my programs, I often receive bold internal knowing. I will always follow this knowing. That said, I am still perfectly capable of going cold with fear, thinking I am horribly mistaken. Yet I *will* walk forward. My inner voice of love has never steered me wrong. My friend Susan once put it this way years ago: "You are a doubting Tama. You question everything. And you are the most faithful person I have ever met."

When I first got the written contract for this book from the publisher of my dreams, the working title of the book was *Trusting Yourself Deeply*. The contract read: "To Tama Kieves for 'Trusting Yourself Deeply.'" When I first read it as a single sentence, it felt *like a message to me*. I began to cry. This was a sorcerer's wink, a bow and a nod for all these years of staying on my own crazy, brave path and guiding others to theirs.

When I finished writing this book, I felt clear, as though the balm of eucalyptus surged through my veins. I was a woman who had scraped her way to the top of her mountain and praised the day. The incredible Maya Angelou once shared, "Wouldn't take nothing for my journey now." I knew what she meant. I knew I had been "writing what wants to be written," the maxim I teach in all my writing classes. It is a feeling of *recognition* to allow the current of your larger self to course through you.

But then my monkey mind started in on me. My dearest wish is that this book finds its readers—and *maybe* that they have friends, or networks of influence. So, naturally, having readers is where my inner worrier focused. *What if no one relates to this book? What if no one wants to learn about trusting themselves? Maybe that's not what's on their minds?*

I scribbled these questions in my journal on a plane. Immediately,

I hungered for reassurance. I am a just a little bit needy when it comes to my love affair with the Universe. I bet there's a whole department in the ether dedicated to calming down the Mexican jumping beans in my brain—and finding new ways to encourage my faith.

I have to tell you: right after I wrote those questions in my journal, this is what happened. I had flown in to lead a retreat at the famous Kripalu Center. The same afternoon I arrived, I sat on the scenic grounds and recorded a quick video for my Instagram and Facebook followers. The second I finished recording, a young woman approached me shyly. "Will you help me?" she said. "I know you teach here, and I think I need to talk to you."

She told me how she was in a program and wasn't feeling as though she'd gotten the answer she needed from the facilitator or group. We talked for a bit, and as I took in the details of her story I said, "Maybe you need to slow down a bit. Maybe this is your time to heal instead of rushing out and doing things." The woman immediately burst into tears.

"That's the exact answer that was coming to me during the retreat," she said. "I didn't trust it, though, because everyone else was finding these great next steps." She looked at me in amazement. "I had my answer the whole time. I just didn't trust myself." She grew quiet and strong, and I could swear she looked ten years younger. Then she looked straight at me with glowing eyes. "Maybe I need to learn to trust myself," she said.

My eyes glowed right back at her. Because I knew she had received her answer. And I had received mine. "Yes," I said. "Learning to trust yourself is a great idea."

32

Let's Stay Connected

TAMAKIEVES.COM
connect@tamakieves.com
MEDIA: tamakieves.com/tama-in-the-media
BOOK FOR SPEAKING: tamakieves.com/book-tama-to-speak
INSTAGRAM: @tamakieves
FACEBOOK: TamaKievesAuthor
LINKEDIN: tamakieves
YOUTUBE: @TamaKieves

Join our global community of maverick spirits through
my programs and social media.

**Trusting your inner genius is worth everything.
It deserves support.**

HERE ARE A FEW WAYS TO DIVE DEEPER:

- **JOIN MY NEXT LIVE CLASS:** I offer online and in-person workshops on Learning to Trust Yourself, Unleash Your Calling, *A Course in Miracles,* Writing Breakthroughs, and more.
- **GET COACHED:** Single sessions and packages to help you rock your brilliance, and group coaching. Looking to help others? Check out my coach training program.

- **HOST A BOOK CLUB/DISCUSSION GROUP:** Coaches, therapists, and spiritual groups, have at it! There are great suggestions and guidelines for you in the **Trust Yourself Mega Pack,** the free companion to this book on page 312.
- **ATTEND A RETREAT:** Fast-track your growth in inspiring locations, immersing yourself in great energy, experiential exercises, and a new way of seeing your life.
- **FOLLOW ME ON SOCIAL MEDIA:** Engage, reflect, and share your thoughts. I love listening and conversing with you. I do livestreams—and look for my podcast!
- **EXPLORE FREE RESOURCES:** Access articles, coaching videos, and virtual events. Don't miss the free **Trust Yourself Mega Pack,** a companion to this book, on page 312 to deepen your self-trust.

IF YOU LOVED THIS BOOK . . .

I want to hear from you. My life's work has taught me that the right people always find each other. The right speaking opportunities, creative collaborations, and work soulmates come together, and our connection benefits the world. **If you are feeling called to be part of the inspired revolution of helping others to trust themselves and their highest resources, contact me.** Magic doesn't happen in isolation. I would love your help in spreading awareness of this work. I believe in word of mouth and word of heart. No effort is too small or too great. You never know who you can touch. Let us all be part of the sacred web of progress.

Everything good that has ever happened to me has happened through great people reaching out. I hope that's you.

POSSIBLE SUGGESTIONS

- INVITE ME TO SPEAK: I can tailor the book's messages for your organization or group through interactive keynotes, presentations, or workshops.
- WRITE A REVIEW: Share your thoughts about this book on your platform or favorite retail site.
- BE AN AMBASSADOR: Suggest me to your favorite podcast, show, or media contacts you think need to know about this book.

Trust yourself, amazing one. Each of us has our role to play in creating the world we wish to live in. Follow your inner genius. I will follow mine. And perhaps our paths will cross.

33

Bonus Resources

TRUST YOURSELF MEGA PACK

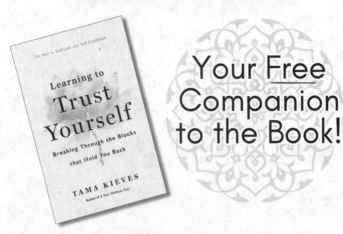

Your Free Companion to the Book!

FREE TOOLS FOR TRUSTING YOURSELF AND YOUR LIFE

Trusting yourself takes practice. Here's a curated collection of videos, meditations, and other materials to support your journey:

- **Inspired Self Dialogue to Undo Fear:** Video Instruction of My Best Practice.
- **The Essence of *A Course in Miracles* Video:** A power principle you can use right now.
- **Immersive Guided Audio Meditation:** "Meeting Your Strength."
- **Printable Self-Trust Codes:** Beautiful, shareable copies from the book.
- **Digital Fortune Cookies and Monthly Mojo Messages:** Wisdom in your inbox.
- **Free Pass for the Inspired & Unstoppable Life Tribe:** Life-changing support for creating the work and life you love.
- **Book Group Guide:** Great suggestions for starting and guiding a *Learning to Trust Yourself* group.

IT'S ALL HERE FOR YOU! AND IT'S ALL FREE.
Get Everything with One Click at:

www.tamakieves.com/trust-yourself-resources

Acknowledgments

First, I would like to acknowledge *you,* the reader. With all my heart I thank you. I wrote this book on the faith that you would find it—and here you are. In a complex, we-are-all-interconnected way, you were part of helping me write this book.

To my Inspired & Unstoppable Life Tribe and my *A Course in Miracles* groups, please take this in: this book exists because of you. Our community moves me. You taught me who I am by letting me teach you who you are. I'm miraculously grateful. Now go rock the world and make your Tama proud.

Joel Fotinos: If there is any one person I acknowledge in this book, it is you. I am so grateful for our soul connection. I love you dearly and for all time. I am also so grateful for our professional connection: your quick intelligence, laser focus, and commitment to being "the reader police." I know this book has clarity and structure (not to mention a title) it never would have had, but for you. Thank you, thank you, thank you for helping me so profoundly to do my life's work. You are one of the biggest reasons I trust in a loving Universe.

Marney Makridakis: Holy crap. I do not even want to imagine where I would have been without your friendship, brilliance, and contribution to my work in the world. Who knew it was even possible to love someone wildly, work with them, snort-laugh with them through crises, write "Darleen Notes," and more. Thank you for sharing every texture of this journey with me.

Paul Kuhn, my life partner: Thank you for always seeing me as "world class" and for dragging suitcases with me up the subway steps, standing in our truth that "there is no world," and so much more. You are strong, brave, and made of holy molecules. There is no one in the world like you. You know me. I'm a treasure hunter. That's why I chose you.

Team TAMA: To Pepper, the firecracker who broke the spell; Alanna, the goddess of pure help and kindness; Karena, the generous soul and Instagram Snake Charmer. And to Marney, Paul, and everyone else . . . thank you for helping me reach the thousands of souls we reach and helping them trust themselves and create exceptional lives.

Inner Team TAMA: Ann Strong, Grace Welker, Sylvaine Hughson, Robin Mower, SARK, I am so grateful to share our lives together. Our conversations and soul-tending keep me trusting myself.

My parents: I have written about my mother a lot in this book, and my father too. I chose memories or stories that fit the teaching piece I was writing. But here's what I didn't say: I love them deeply. My mother is part of me. And if she's reading this from the other realm, I want to say thank you, Mommy, for everything. I hope you are dancing. And if my father is reading this from the other realm, I'd beam at him with so much love and say: you were such an amazing soul, even while troubled. I am so much like you, Daddy, in the best ways, and I am so proud of that.

To all mavericks and teachers past, present, and to come: I am so thankful for messengers who make our world a better place. I can't possibly list all the resources that have supported me, but these are a few influences that were present as I wrote this book: *A Course in Miracles,* Abraham Hicks, Pema Chödrön, Anne Lamott, Anita Moorjani, Ally Boothroyd, East Forest music, *The*

Sun magazine, the Omega Institute, the Kripalu Center for Yoga and Health, Black Swan yoga, Mixture candles, Republic of Tea's Orange Ginger Mint tea, and pistachios from Sprouts market. And to dogs everywhere.

Finally, I owe absolutely everything to my beloved inner teacher.

About the Author

© Jason Johnson

TAMA KIEVES, an honors graduate of Harvard Law School, left her law practice with a prestigious law firm to write and to help others live their most extraordinary lives. She's the author of:

- *This Time I Dance! Creating the Work You Love*
- *Inspired & Unstoppable: Wildly Succeeding in Your Life's Work!*
- *A Year Without Fear: 365 Days of Magnificence*
- *Thriving Through Uncertainty*
- *A Course in Miracles for Life Ninjas*

Featured in *USA Today,* Oprah media, and other national outlets, she is a sought-after speaker and visionary career/success coach who has helped thousands worldwide to discover and thrive in the life, work, and business of their dreams.

Tama has presented at TEDx and is on the faculty of premier holistic venues. She is known for her electrifying presence, grounded compassion, and dynamic sense of humor, as well as the sweeping possibilities she ignites in others. She has also taught *A Course in Miracles* in a highly experiential way for more than thirty years.

From Brooklyn, New York, Tama now lives under the blue skies of Denver, Colorado. Visit her online at TamaKieves.com. She would love it if you did!